GIANTS
IN THE
SKY

GIANTS IN THE SKY

MICHAEL J.H. TAYLOR
and DAVID MONDEY

JANE'S

First published in 1982 by
Jane's Publishing Company Limited
238 City Road, London EC1V 2PU

ISBN 0 7106 0190 5

Computer typesetting by
Method Limited, Woodford Green, Essex

Printed in Great Britain by
Biddles Limited, Guildford, Surrey

CONTENTS

INTRODUCTION

A glance at a fairly comprehensive dictionary will confirm for you that there are several definitions of the word giant. Primary, of course, is the generally accepted meaning of giant in proportions, so you will find in the following pages a comprehensive selection of the world's very large aircraft, including the Hughes H-4 Hercules, the 'daddy of them all'.

But giant also has connotations relating to achievement and capability, which accounts for the inclusion of aircraft in the class of the MacCready Solar Challenger. This, although very small by comparison with some of the heavier and lighter-than-air craft included in this book, recorded on 7 July 1981 the first solar-powered flight across the English Channel, which is a far from insignificant achievement.

Our list of 100 aircraft was compiled with the foregoing comments in mind, and the aim has been not only to include the mammoths among civil and military types, but also a selection of the craft that are giants in achievement or capability. We believe that they help to highlight some of the important milestones in aviation's exciting and colourful history.

M.J.H.T. and D.M. 1981

AEG
R.I

Germany

Allgemeine Elektrizitäts Gesellschaft, best remembered for its twin-engined G type bombers of 1915-18, also attempted to emulate Zeppelin Staaken and others in producing a giant R type heavy bomber. Although AEG themselves described the R.I as a normal tractor biplane, it was hardly that. For a start the four 194 kW (260 hp) Mercedes D IVa engines were mounted in the fuselage fore and aft, with a 70 cm (2 ft 3 in) gap between the pairs. Power from these to the two propellers was transmitted through single leather cone clutches to a common main gear above the engines, from which two shafts led to reduction gears with reduced rpm from 1,450 to 750. The

engine room was partitioned off by sliding doors, in front of which was an observer cabin with unhindered views forward, sideways and downward. On top of the cabin was a machine-gun position. To the rear of the engine room a gangway led through a large cabin with a gun position to the open pilot's cockpit aft of the wings.

The wings themselves had no stagger or sweepback, the lower planes only having any dihedral. The angle of incidence was 5° to the outer struts, from which point it decreased almost to nothing at the tip, giving the wingtips a twisted look. Steel tubes and wires were used exclusively for the body and wing framework; the wing main spars were of chrome nickel tubes and the ribs were duralumin girder types. The forward portion of the body to rear of the engine room was covered with plywood, thereafter with fabric.

The R.I giant bomber broke up in the air on 3 September 1918, probably because of propeller failure. Unfortunately, all the crew were killed, including the designer Lt Bruchmann.

AEG R.I.

AERO SPACELINES
Guppy-201

USA

Established at Santa Barbara, California, Aero Spacelines was responsible for the construction of a series of giant aircraft that must be regarded as some of the strangest to be seen in our modern skies. Their development originated when this company realised there could be a requirement for specialised transport aircraft that would be suitable for the carriage of outsize sections of hardware. The original concept related to such items as the booster rockets being used in US space programmes, and as a private venture the company initiated two conversions of Boeing Stratocruiser/C-97 transport aircraft under the new names Pregnant Guppy and Super Guppy respectively.

Following completion of these two aircraft, and subsequent demonstration of their unique cargo

Aero Spacelines Guppy-201
Right: Aero Spacelines Guppy-201 displaying its swing-nose (*Ugo Sbaragua*)

capability, the US government contracted for the exclusive use of these two aircraft for NASA and the US Department of Defense. This led Aero Spacelines to the conclusion that there ought to be a commercial requirement for the transport of large assemblies, and resulting in the development of three more members of this Guppy family, of which the largest is the Guppy-201.

This derives from the use of existing B-377/C-97 airframes, with portions of the lower fuselage of several of these aircraft being united to provide the basis of the much larger cabin. Above this, and accounting for the whale-like proportions of the completed aircraft, the company designed and built a huge circular-section 'bubble' structure over the top of the newly-configured lower fuselage, and ultimately providing a cargo hold with a maximum width and height of 7.65 m (25 ft 1 in) and 7.77 m (25 ft 6 in) respectively. The maximum length of this hold is 33.99 m (111 ft 6 in), with the constant-section portion extending for 9.75 m (32 ft). This large volume of cargo space obviously needed something rather better than the average cargo doors to simplify the task of loading and unloading. The solution lay in making it possible for the entire nose structure, forward of the constant-section, to hinge to one side on the ground, supported by the nosewheel unit and a special trolley. This gives completely unobstructed access, with the task

made easier by an air-transportable cargo loader, plus a rail system in the cabin floor, extending for 19.81 m (65 ft), that is able to accommodate oversize pallets. The Guppy-201 retains the flight deck, tail unit, and wings of the C-97, has retractable tricycle landing gear with twin wheels on each unit, and is powered by four Allison 501-D22C turboprops, each rated at 3,663 ekW (4,912 eshp). A closed-circuit television system is provided to enable the crew to monitor the security of the cargo during flight.

The first flight of the original conversion was made on 24 August 1970; and following certification almost exactly a year later, was sold to Airbus Industrie in Europe. A second Guppy-201 was delivered to this manufacturer in September 1973, and these two aircraft have proved to be extremely valuable for the transport of large airframe assemblies for the Airbus production line. This is especially true of the wing assemblies which are manufactured in Britain. Indeed, these aircraft are vital, and with growing production Airbus Industrie has now acquired manufacturing rights for these aircraft from Aero Spacelines. Two more are to be built under sub-contract by UTA Industries of Le Bourget, France, and scheduled for delivery in 1982 and 1983. They will join the two original aircraft, operated for Airbus Industrie by Aeromaritime, a charter subsidiary of UTA.

If you have not seen one of these strange aircraft flying through European skies, your chances of a sighting will be doubled within the next year or so.

Aero Spacelines Super Guppy being used to transport Airbus A300/A310 fuselage sections to the final assembly centre at Toulouse

AIRBUS
A300B

International.

The Airbus A300 wide-bodied transport, designed and produced by a team of European partners, is one of the most exciting current projects of Europe's aerospace industry. Not only is it the only wide-body jetliner to be built on this side of the North Atlantic but, after a nail-biting period when it seemed that a significant number of sales might never materialise, it would now appear to be well on the way to recording a major success for European co-operation. It has been able to demonstrate, over the short-range routes for which it was specifically designed, better operating economics than its rivals from the US, and

this has been a key factor in the growing demand for the Airbus. A healthy order book in the late summer of 1981 showed that despite the delivery of 146 of these aircraft, there were orders and options outstanding for an additional 170. It is a total that is likely to grow as the company continues development of the Airbus to cater for the needs of different airlines, and provide increases in payload/range capability.

The main partners in this co-operative effort are Aérospatiale of France, Deutsche Airbus of West Germany, and British Aerospace in the UK, with contributions coming also from CASA in Spain, Fokker in the Netherlands, and SOKO in Yugoslavia. In addition, subcontracts now, or will, involve manufacturers in Belgium and Italy. The

Airbus A300B4-100 in the livery of Thai Airways International

involvement of the main partners is illustrated by their manufacturing/production responsibilities. Aérospatiale builds the nose section (including flight deck), lower centre fuselage, engine pylons, and is responsible for final assembly at Toulouse. Deutsche Airbus produces the remainder of the forward fuselage, and upper centre/rear fuselage, plus the vertical tail surfaces. British Aerospace is responsible for the basic wing structure, and works in collaboration with Fokker, which produces the wing moving surfaces and wingtips. Last, but by no means least, CASA produces the

Olympic Airways Airbus A300B4

horizontal tail surfaces, and forward passenger and landing gear doors.

Construction of the first A300B1 began in September 1969, and this aircraft made its maiden flight on 28 October 1972. The second, and only other B1, flew initially on 5 February 1973. Current major production version is the A300B4, which entered service with Germanair on 1 June 1975. Its configuration is that of a cantilever mid-wing monoplane, primarily of light alloy construction, but also incorporating some composite materials for secondary structures. The retractable tricycle landing gear has four-wheel main units and a two-wheel nose unit. Power is provided by two advanced technology turbofan engines in the 222.5 kN (50,000 lb st) class. According to customer requirements these may be General Electric CF6-50C/-50C2s, licence-built by SNECMA, or Pratt & Whitney JT9D-59A/-59Bs.

The cabin, which measures 39.15 m (128 ft 6 in) in length, and with a maximum width and height of 5.35 m (17 ft 7 in) and 2.54 m (8 ft 4 in) respectively, is pressurised and air conditioned. It can accommodate 269 passengers in a typical economy class layout, but up to 336 can be carried in a single-class high-density seating arrangement. It is operated normally by a crew of three on the flight deck, and to simplify the task of controlling this big aircraft they have the most advanced avionics equipment available, including a dual automatic landing system.

By any standards the Airbus A300 is an impressive aeroplane, perhaps appreciated most by near-airport dwellers for its comparatively quiet arrivals and departures. When its excellent record to date is added to the company's plans for expansion of its capabilities, there is little doubt that the Airbus will figure prominently in world-wide airline operations for many years to come.

Airbus A300

ANTONOV
An-22

One of the problems that had to be faced by the Soviet Union some twenty years ago, in both civil and military fields, was to find ways and means of carrying large volumes of cargo over very long distances. The solution was not to be found by the use of surface routes, for at that time neither road nor rail could offer the versatility needed. For a nation that had in 1913 created the world's largest aircraft, the Sikorsky Le Grand, it is not surprising that an answer was sought in the sky. In early 1962 Oleg Antonov's bureau was given the task of designing an aircraft suitable for this role, resulting in the An-22. This came as something of a shock to the world's aircraft manufacturers when exhibited at the 1965 Paris Air Show. It was a twofold shock, for not only was it then quite clearly the world's largest operational aircraft, but it had been designed, built, and flown without any knowledge of it leaking out to the other nations of the world.

In fact, the An-22 Antheus, as it became known, had flown for the first time some four months earlier, on 27 February 1965. In configuration it is a cantilever high-wing monoplane, the wing mounted to a fuselage of circular cross-section which is upswept at the rear, and carrying a tail unit that incorporates twin fins and rudders. The retractable tricycle landing gear is designed to be suitable for off-runway operations, and comprises a twin-wheel steerable nose unit, and main units that each consist of three twin-wheel units in tandem. To ensure that cargo space is not in any way compromised by these massive units when the aircraft is in flight, large fairings into which they can retract are built on to each side of the fuselage. These fairings also incorporate a door forward of the wheels, to provide access to the cabin for crew and/or passengers. However, it should not be thought that the Antheus is much concerned with passenger transport, although when it had first been seen at Paris, in 1965, there had been a suggestion that a civil transport version, with seating capacity for some 700 passengers, was to follow.

Cargo carrying is the An-22's primary role, and to enable this to be handled easily a large loading-

Antonov An-22 Antheus (*K.J.A. Brooks*)

ramp/door is provided in the undersurface of the upswept rear fuselage. Retractable jacks, just forward of the hinge-point of the ramp, can be lowered to support the aircraft as heavy items are loaded. And 'heavy' really does mean exactly that, for so far as is known it is still the only Soviet transport aircraft able to airlift the Army's T-62 tank. The load-carrying capability of the An-22 had been demonstrated internationally as early as 1967, when an aircraft with an eight-man crew carried a payload of 100,000 kg (almost 100 tons) to a height of 7,848 m (25,748 ft). But, despite its size, it is certainly not a slow mover, for among other international records that have been gained are a number for speed with payload. As a single example, in 1972 an An-22 captained by Marina Popovich, wife of the Soviet cosmonaut Pavel Popovich, averaged 608.449 km/h (378.073 mph) around a 1,000 km closed circuit, carrying a payload of 50,000 kg (just over 49 tons). Such capability suggests the installation of considerable engine power, and this comprises four 11,186 kW (15,000 shp) Kuznetsov NK-12MA turboprops, each driving two four-blade contra-rotating propellers.

Despite the foregoing some, if not all An-22s, have capacity for a few passengers, for a cabin aft of the flight deck, which is separated from the main cargo hold by a bulkhead with two doors, provides accommodation for 28 or 29. It is believed that about 40 of these giant aircraft were built before deliveries ended during 1974, serving with both the Soviet Air Force and Aeroflot.

Antonov An-22s on manoeuvre (*Tass*)

BARLING
XNBL-1

In most respects the end of the First World War brought a temporary end to the development and production of military aircraft. In the USA, however, there was at least one exception to this generalisation. The impetus that the war had given in the area of research and development was to continue for a short time, fostered by senior officers of the US Army Air Service who realised that both the service, and the nation's aircraft industry, still needed to learn a great deal about the design and development of military aeroplanes. In particular, the Air Service was anxious to develop a strategic bombing capability, but its early efforts in this direction, of which the Barling XNBL-1 represented just one attempt, were not crowned with success. Designed by British engineer, Walter Barling, who was then employed by the USAAS Engineering Division, based at McCook Field, Ohio, the XNBL-1 (Experimental Night Bomber Long-range) was built in sections by the Witteman-Lewis Aircraft Corporation of Newark, New Jersey.

Its configuration was that of an extensively strutted and braced triplane, the mid-wing of reduced span and chord by comparison with the upper and lower wings, each of which spanned 36.58 m (120 ft). The XNBL-1 was, understandably, the world's largest aeroplane at the time of its construction. The fuselage was a conventional

Barling XNBL-1

semi-monocoque structure, built in sections, and mounting a biplane tail unit that incorporated no fewer than four fins and rudders, the fins serving also as interplane struts for the biplane horizontal surfaces. The incidence of the entire tail unit could be adjusted in flight, a capability that, reportedly, was a difficult engineering problem to resolve at that time. Equally unusual was the tailskid landing gear, each main unit comprising four wheels with tyres of 1.52 m (5 ft) diameter, plus two wheels strut-mounted beneath the fuselage nose to prevent any tendency of the aircraft to 'nose-over' when landing on rough ground. A control in the cockpit enabled the pilot to extend the two forward wheels of each main unit for landing. These had long-stroke oil shock-absorbers, and took the first landing loads: as the speed dropped off and the tail came down, the aircraft settled also on the rear main wheels (with rubber-in-compression shock-absorption) and the tail skid.

Power was provided by six 313 kW (420 hp) Liberty inline engines. These were strut-mounted between the lower and mid-wings, the inboard installation on each side comprising two engines, back-to-back, and driving tractor and pusher propellers. In the outboard position on each side was a single engine, driving a tractor propeller. Accommodation was provided for two pilots, side by side, with dual controls. Five positions mounted a total of seven machine-guns, to allow a wide field of defensive fire.

First flown on 22 August 1923, by Lts Harold R. Harris and Muir Fairchild, the XNBL-1 was to prove a great disappointment. For while there were no control problems (despite having ailerons only on the upper wings), it was so seriously underpowered that it failed to attain a speed of 161 km/h (100 mph), and was unable to overfly the Appalachian Mountains during a trip from Dayton to Washington. Prior to initial tests, C.G. Grey had written in *Jane's All the World's Aircraft:*. . . 'Specifications require that not more than 5,000 lb of bombs shall be carried at one time, but were anything so large as a 10,000 lb bomb developed, the Barling could lift and fly it for two hours'. Such hoped-for ideals could not be attained, and in 1925 further development of the XNBL-1 was abandoned. An improved XNBL-2 had been planned, but a lack of funds, as well as of confidence in the development of such an aircraft, meant that it was many years before the US Army Air Corps was to hold in its inventory an aircraft anywhere near as big as the Barling bomber.

BEARDMORE
Inflexible

UK

During the First World War William Beardmore and Co, a firm of engineers and shipbuilders, produced aircraft under licence as well as a number of machines of its own design, notably the SB.3 (W.B.III) Sopwith Pup development.

Beardmore Inflexible

After the Armistice it designed a series of commercial aircraft, but the state of the market was such that in 1921 it ceased aircraft development. However, in 1924 the aircraft department was reopened and work began on a two-seat lightplane for an Air Ministry competition.

Also in 1924 Beardmore acquired rights to the German Rohrbach methods of metal construction, with the result that it soon delivered the Inverness to the RAF for testing, a twin-engined all-metal monoplane flying-boat. Beardmore followed this with the Inflexible, the first aircraft to be built entirely by the Beardmore company and remembered as the largest British landplane up to the Second World War. Designed as an experimental bomber, the Inflexible was powered by three 484 kW (650 hp) Rolls-Royce Condor II engines, one in the nose and two under the huge cantilever wings. Apart from the steel fittings, this bomber was built entirely of duralumin, and practically throughout the aircraft the metal was used in the form of flat, or nearly flat, sheets or plates, riveted together. The landing gear was also of unusual type, with enormous single wheels on each main unit and a smaller tailwheel.

The Inflexible took to the air for the first time on 5 March 1928, and in RAF markings it received the serial number J7557, although it had been built under the reserved civil registration G-EBNG. Despite its size, it was found to handle well and was responsive to the controls, but, nevertheless, it remained a prototype.

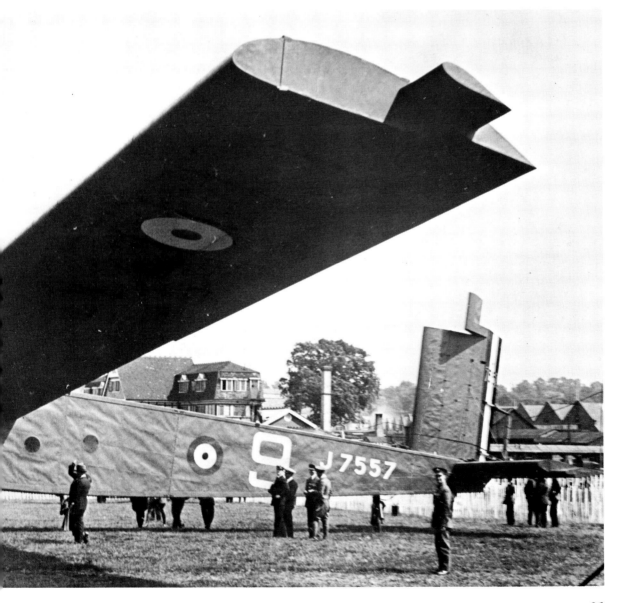

BLACKBURN
B-101 Beverley

UK

General Aircraft Ltd, established originally at Croydon in 1931, began in 1945 to study the design of large transport aircraft that would have both civil and military applications. The company considered that its experience, gained from design and production of the Hamilcar (q.v.) assault glider during the war years, would prove valuable in formulating a practical design. Thus, when in due course the Air Ministry issued Specification C.3/46, calling for a medium-range tactical transport, the company was well advanced in its thinking, and able to develop a design that was sufficiently attractive to win a contract for the

construction of a prototype. Identified by the company as the G.A.L.60, and named Universal Freighter to signify that it was suitable for both civil and military use, this flew for the first time on 20 June 1950, by which time General Aircraft had merged with Blackburn Aircraft Ltd to form Blackburn and General Aircraft Ltd.

The general configuration of the G.A.L.60 comprised a deep fuselage that would be able to accommodate two tiers of vehicles, terminating in a large tailboom with a high-mounted tailplane and elevators at the aft end, and with large endplate fins and rudders. The cantilever monoplane wing was also set high on the fuselage, mounting four engines in leading-edge nacelles, and having attached beneath the wing the stalky main units of the non-retractable tricycle landing gear. These units, each carrying a four-wheel bogie, were braced to the fuselage at their lower end by horizontal sponsons.

In an endeavour to secure orders for civil variants, the company put up a proposal to Silver City Airways for a cross-Channel car ferry version that would accommodate six cars on two

Blackburn Beverley of No 30 Squadron, RAF, unloading a lorry in Kuwait, 1961

main fuselage decks, plus 42 passengers in a modified tailboom that would be redesigned to serve as a passenger cabin. Nothing was to come of this, but the idea of utilising the tail boom was retained for use in the aircraft that were ordered for delivery to RAF Transport Command in 1955. The second prototype, incorporating a number of modifications, and known to the company as the Blackburn and General Type 65 Universal Mk 2, served as the prototype of the RAF Beverley, flown for the first time in June 1953. Just over 18 months later, on 29 January 1955, the first production Beverley C.Mk 1 was flown, the first of 47 to be built for the RAF, these serving with Nos.30,34,47,53 and 84 Squadrons. At that time it was the largest aircraft to have entered service with the RAF.

In the finalised production version, power was provided by four Bristol Centaurus 173 radial engines, each developing 2,125 kW (2,850 hp) for take-off with water/methanol injection. During flight, access could be gained to equipment mounted within the engine nacelles via wing crawlways. The main freight compartment was 12.19 m (40 ft) long, with a maximum width and height of 3.05 m (10 ft), and it was enclosed at the rear end by a pair of clamshell doors: these could be removed for dropping operations, and the hinged loading ramps at the rear of the freight floor could also be removed when not required. Typical loads included 94 troops or 70 paratroops, of which 36 and 30 respectively were accommodated in the tailboom cabin. In an ambulance role 48 stretchers could be carried in the main compartment, plus 34 ambulatory casualties in the tailboom. In addition, a heavy drop platform retaining and release gear made it possible to airdrop single loads of up to 11,340 kg (25,000 lb), and in October 1959 one of these aircraft dropped an 18,144 kg (40,000 lb) military load suspended by eight parachutes, then representing the largest load dropped from an aircraft in the UK. The type gave approximately ten years of service before being withdrawn from use at the end of 1967.

Blackburn Beverley of No 30 Squadron, RAF

Blackburn Beverley (*Charles E. Brown*)

BLOHM UND VOSS
Bv 222 Wiking

Germany

Design of the Blohm und Voss Bv 222, which was to prove the largest flying-boat of any nation to see operational service in the Second World War, began in the late 1930s to provide Deutsche Lufthansa with a long-range flying-boat that would be suitable for transatlantic services. Designed by a team under the leadership of Richard Vogt, the large hull was of all-metal construction, and carried a cantilever tail unit aft. Of particularly interesting design was the all-metal cantilever monoplane wing, its large-diameter tubular steel spar serving not only to function as a wing spar, but also to carry the mountings for the combined power plant of six radial engines, housed in leading-edge nacelles. It was also compartmented to provide fuel and oil tanks for these engines. Retractable stabilising floats were mounted beneath each wing, each unit comprising two half-floats that were hinged to move away from each other when retracted to lie within wing recesses.

As designed originally for service with Deutsche Lufthansa, this flying-boat was intended to accommodate 24 passengers, but by the time that the prototype Bv 222V-1 (D-ANTE) made its maiden flight on 7 September 1940 the nation was already involved in the Second World War. Without doubt, this meant that deployment of the new 'boat in its intended role would not be possible, and because of this an evaluation programme was initiated to ascertain the suitability of the Bv 222 for military applications. Early tests proved its capability as a long-range transport for both personnel and cargo, and to make it easier to load the latter the hull was modified to include larger loading doors. With this work completed, and without any defensive armament, the Bv 222V-1 was used operationally for the first time on 10 July 1941, carrying freight to northern Norway. Soon afterwards, it was switched to a trans-Mediterranean route, busy carrying supplies for the Afrika Korps, a task which despite the lack of armament was not really hazardous when its usual fighter escorts were in attendance. However, on odd occasions a rendez-vous with the escorts failed, resulting in a somewhat dicey operation that could eventually have only one end. Accordingly, the Bv 222V-1 was withdrawn from service for the installation of armament, comprising five MG 81 7.9 mm machine-guns in nose and waist positions, plus two MG 131 13 mm guns, each in an upper turret. So modified, the aircraft was handed over to the specially-formed Lufttransportstaffel See 222, which had been established to control the operation of the large 'boats. When used as a troop transport 92 fully-equipped troops could be accommodated, or up to 72 stretchers in a casualty evacuation role. The second prototype, which had flown for the first time on 7 August 1941, and was earmarked for service with the Fliegerführer Atlantik, carried armament from the beginning. This was similar to that installed in Bv 222V-1, but included also four more MG 131 machine-guns, these mounted in pairs in two

Blohm und Voss Bv 222 Wiking (*Bundesarchiv*)

gondolas beneath the wing centre-section. This installation was later removed when it was discovered that the gondolas considerably reduced performance, and following the completion of this work the Bv 222V-2 was delivered to the LTS See 222, joining the first prototype, instead of going to the FF Atlantik.

By 1943 seven prototypes (Bv 222V-1 to 6, and Bv 222V-8) had been delivered to LTS See 222. Three were lost during operations in the Mediterranean, two destroyed by enemy fighters, and the remaining four were converted for a maritime reconnaissance role and transferred to the FF Atlantik.

Power plant of the early aircraft had consisted of six 746 kW (1,000 hp) BMW/Bramo Fafnir 323R radial engines, and aircraft so equipped were designated Bv 222A by the Luftwaffe. The installation of six 746 kW (1,000 hp) Junkers Jumo 207C diesel engines in the Bv 222V-7

prototype was regarded as highly effective, with a decision being made to standardise on a diesel power plant installation. However, a decision by Junkers to discontinue development of the Jumo diesel brought this plan to an end.

Production of these giant Blohm und Voss flying-boats was to end during 1944, after only 13 had been built (including the nine prototypes). This was due to the need to ensure that available strategic materials were used for the production of essential bomber and fighter aircraft. Thus, there were only four true production Bv 222Cs, but it is interesting to record that examples of these 'boats that were used in a maritime reconnaissance role carried FuG 200 Hohentwiel search radar, and FuG 216R Neptun equipment to give warning of attack from the rear. Only three of the Wikings survived the war; two of them were tested subsequently in the USA, and one (Bv 222C-012) in the UK.

BLOHM UND VOSS
Bv 238

Germany

Shortly after completion of basic design of the Bv 222, Richard Vogt's design team began work on a large flying-boat project which also stemmed from a Deutsche Lufthansa requirement. This was not to be realised because of the outbreak of war and, in fact, this early cancellation seemed to set a seal of failure on the idea of producing a 'boat of this class.

The design team turned instead to a requirement of the Reichsluftfahrtministerium (RLM) for a large general purpose flying-boat, desired as an ultimate replacement for the Bv 138s which became operational in the autumn of 1940. In its original design layout, this was to have been powered by four Junkers Jumo 223 diesel engines of 1,864 kW (2,500 hp), but when it was realised that these were unlikely to materialise, this design also was scrapped.

In order to arrive at a combined power plant with a similar total maximum output, it was decided to use six engines of around 1,268 kW (1,700 hp), and resulted in the idea of developing what would virtually be an enlarged version of the Bv 222. This plan appealed to the RLM, possibly because the enlargement of an existing design seemed less likely to result in development delays, and four prototypes were ordered. The first three were to be powered by 1,305 kW (1,750 hp) Daimler Benz liquid-cooled engines, and leading to a production Bv 238A. The fourth

Blohm und Voss Bv 238 (*Deutsches Museum, Munich*)

would evaluate BMW radial air-cooled engines and, if proving more effective, would result in development of a production version designated Bv 238B.

Although of generally similar configuration to the Bv 222, the hull design of the new 'boat introduced some advanced hydrodynamic proposals and, to discover whether these were practical before incorporating them in the giant hull of the prototype, it was decided to build a flying model with dimensions that were approximately one quarter of full size. Work on this was entrusted to a company with some experience of wooden glider construction, but the resulting FG-227, as it was designated, was not ready for testing until early 1944. Built near Prague, the model was sabotaged as it was being entrained for transport to Germany, and the necessary repairs were not completed until September of that year. Then, when the FG-227 was eventually flown for the first time, a fuel system failure stopped all six engines, and the little flying-boat was severely damaged in the resulting forced landing. All in all, an expensive exercise which provided no information.

Construction of the prototypes proceeded, however, during which time wing span and area were increased to allow for the installation of wing-mounted gun-turrets. In fact, no armament was incorporated in the Bv 238V-1, which began flight tests in the spring of 1944. Before initial testing was completed on the Schaal See (or Schaal lake), to the West of Scherin, the flying-boat was destroyed at its moorings by strafing Mustangs of the USAAF. None of the remaining prototypes were completed before the war's end, and the Bv 238's only claim to fame resulted from the fact that it was the largest flying-boat to be built and flown by any nation during the Second World War.

BOEING
B-29/B-50 Superfortress

USA

When the US Army Air Force became involved in the Second World War following the Japanese attack on Pearl Harbor, it included in its inventory the Boeing B-17 Flying Fortress which, for its day, could be numbered among the world's giant aircraft. Ranking paramount in its bomber force at the end of that war was another giant from the same stable, the Boeing B-29 Superfortress, development of which had started in early 1940 to meet the USAAF's requirement for a 'Hemisphere Defense Weapon'. Agreed, it is a curious procurement description for a strategic bomber. It illustrates the subterfuge then needed in isolationist America (at that date not involved in the war raging in Europe) to initiate the development of what would prove to be essential weapons. If the nation, and its political leaders, believed that the policy of isolation could survive a major European war, military planners were rather more realistic. They knew also that an advanced weapon, such as that called for by the 1940 specification, could not be developed overnight.

The official requirement was for a maximum speed of 644 km/h (400 mph), armour, self-sealing fuel tanks, heavy defensive armament, a 7,257 kg (16,000 lb) bombload, and the ability to carry 907 kg (2,000 lb) of bombs for some 8,500 km (5,300 miles). Boeing's proposed Model 345 was selected by the USAAF, from submissions that included those from Consolidated, Douglas and Lockheed, and the first XB-29 prototype was

Boeing B-29 Superfortress

Boeing B-29A Superfortress

flown for the first time on 21 September 1942. By then, of course, the USA was well and truly involved in the war, both in Europe and the Pacific, and the B-29 had become a high-priority requirement. The result was that production of this big bomber, which had presented problems in its initial procurement, was to total more than 3,900 examples.

The original specification had been a little ambitious, and the B-29 never did quite attain such lofty ideals, but it more than lived up to the hopes of the USAAF planners that had fought and argued for so long to obtain what they considered to be an essential weapon. Of mid-wing mono-

plane configuration, the B-29 was powered by four 1,641 kW (2,200 hp) Wright R-3350 turbo-charged radial engines. Its crew was accommodated in two main pressurised compartments, interconnected by a tunnel that passed above the bomb bay. The tail gunner's position was also pressurised, but access was possible only when the pressurisation system was off. Armament varied a little, but the basic installation comprised two 0.50 in machine-guns in each of four remotely-controlled gun turrets plus, and according to version, a 20mm cannon and two machine-guns, or three machine-guns in the tail turret. The maximum bombload was 9,072 kg (20,000 lb). The B-29 is remembered as the aircraft which dropped the atomic bombs on the Japanese cities

Boeing B-29A Superfortress *Look Homeward Angel* on Bolo Strip, Okinawa, having been damaged by flak on 11 August 1945 (*US Air Force*)

Boeing KB-29P tanker refuelling a B-50D Superfortress bomber by 'flying-boom'

of Hiroshima and Nagasaki in August 1945. However, before this, on the night of 9/10 March 1945, a force of 334 B-29s had launched an incendiary attack on Tokyo, during which almost 84,000 people lost their lives. In the early post-war years the Superfortress was to see service for air/sea rescue, flight refuelling, photo-reconnaissance, and weather reconnaissance, and were last used in a bomber role during the Korean War.

This, however, is not quite the end of the B-29 story, for a version with 2,610 kW (3,500 hp) Pratt & Whitney R-4360 Wasp Major radial

engines had been planned. Other changes included a strengthened but lighter-weight wing structure, increased fin and rudder area, and improved landing gear for operation at higher weights. Originally designated B-29D, this entered production in early 1945, being redesignated as the B-50 before any were delivered. First examples went to the USAF in late 1947, and several variants were to enter service with Strategic Air Command. Most easily recognised was the B-50D with large underwing auxiliary fuel tanks, and the KB-50J/-50K flight refuelling tankers with a General Electric J87-GE-23 auxiliary turbojet engine beneath each wing to boost the maximum speed. A few of these tankers remained in service in 1965, operating in Vietnam.

BOEING
B-52 Stratofortress

USA

The B-52 Stratofortress, which despite its age remains one of the three major strategic deterrents of the United States in 1981, began to take shape on Boeing drawing boards almost immediately after the Second World War had ended. The USAAF was then showing interest in the development of a turbine-powered long-range bomber, and an Air Force design competition was initiated in 1946 to gain submissions from the nation's aircraft industry. This resulted in Boeing being awarded a contract to finalise design details, and leading in July 1948 to the company gaining a contract for the construction of two prototypes.

One of the biggest problems posed by the requirement related to the selection of suitable power plant. The company had no doubt that turbojets were essential if the aircraft was to have the kind of performance that would help to ensure survivability in a hostile environment. Unfortunately, turbojets of that era were extremely fuel-thirsty, leading to a decision to use turboprops which were far more economical in operation. This marked the beginning of a

The huge eight-engined Boeing B-52G Stratofortress carrying SRAM missiles

chaotic and frustrating period, when seemingly endless meetings were held to try and finalise engine selection and layout. It was resolved only when Pratt & Whitney decided in 1949 to proceed with development of the J57 turbojet, a feature of its design being a new two-spool compressor that promised greater fuel economy.

In its final design form, the B-52 had many points of similarity with the USAF's B-47 medium-range bomber, which had entered service some ten months before the first YB-52 prototype was flown on 15 April 1952, followed by the XB-52 prototype on 2 October 1952. The B-52 is a cantilever high-wing monoplane, with 35° wing sweepback and a very thin aerofoil section. Landing gear is of bicycle type, with four twin-wheel main units in tandem pairs, and these can be castored for a crosswind take-off or landing. They are complemented by small outrigger units, retracting into the wing undersurface outboard

of the outer engines. Power plant comprises eight J57 turbojets, pylon-mounted in pairs beneath the wing leading-edges, and pressurised accommodation is provided for a crew of six.

Production of the first B-52As totalled only three, these being used by the company for test and development. First to enter service was the B-52B with 44.5 kN (10,000 lb st) J57s, and it was an aircraft of this version which dropped the first known airborne hydrogen bomb over Bikini Atoll, on 21 May 1956. Of the 50 B-52Bs that were built, 27 were converted to reconnaissance RB-52Bs.

YB-52 prototype with a tandem cockpit for the pilots, standing beside the once large B-17 Flying Fortress bomber

Right: **YB-52 in flight, showing clearly the tandem cockpit arrangement**

Following versions have included the B-52C with improvements in performance and equipment; the B-52D with an improved fire-control system for the tail guns; B-52E with a new flight deck layout, more advanced navigation equipment, and a new weapons system; and the B-52F which introduced higher output J57-P-43 engines, each of which developed 49.8 kN (11,200 lb st).

The B-52F was followed by the considerably improved B-52G, which it had been intended should be the last production version. The addition of integral wing and fixed underwing fuel tanks gave much increased range; the tail turret was converted to remote control, its gunner moved forward into the crew compartment; and a reduced-height fin of increased chord was introduced. Armament included two new AGM-28 Hound Dog stand-off missiles, one carried beneath each wing, making this version of the B-52 the first stage of a very-long-range missile system. There was, however, to be one more 'final' version, the B-52H. This introduced the 75.6 kN (17,000 lb st) and more fuel-efficient Pratt & Whitney TF33-P-3 turbofan; structural changes to make low-level penetration flights possible with reduced fatigue; a Gatling gun in the tail turret to replace machine-guns; equipment to carry and launch Quail ECM decoy missiles, carried in the weapons bay; and provisions to carry beneath the wing the Skybolt ballistic missile, that failed to become operational. When the last of the B-52Hs came off the production line a total of 744 of these big and potent bombers had been built.

Later alternative programmes to the B-52 have failed to materialise and, as a result, 347 B-52D/G/Hs remained operational in 1981, with an additional 187 B-52s retained in inactive storage. Those which remain in service have been, and are being, continually updated with very advanced avionics equipment. This will make it possible for them to remain a very formidable strategic aircraft over a period which could last until the end of the present century. (q.v. Rockwell International B-1B)

One of three Boeing B-52 Stratofortress bombers that flew non-stop around the world during 16-18 January 1957

BOEING
Model 314

USA

As described in the XB-15 entry, constructional and other data obtained from the bomber programme was used in the design of later military aircraft. Interestingly, wings and tail surfaces similar to those used on the XB-15 were employed also on the Model 314, a highly successful commercial flying-boat.

In 1935 Pan American Airways decided to purchase a fleet of very large flying-boats for transatlantic and other services. In the following year Boeing received an order for six, to be known as Clippers. XB-15-type wings and tail surfaces were married to a new semi-monocoque hull with cantilever hydro-stabilisers. The hull was divided into eleven sections by bulkheads, and included a flight deck, a main passenger deck, and a series of watertight compartments below the floor structure. On the flight deck was accommodated the crew of six, which did not include the two stewards, while 74 passengers occupied the main deck. The standard passenger compartments were convertible into sleeping units with upper and lower berths for 40 passengers if required. Passenger comfort was assured by the inclusion of a special dining saloon, galley, separate dressing rooms and toilets, and a private drawing room. But even with all this, the Model 314 still had space for 4,763 kg (10,500 lb) of highly-profitable mail or cargo.

Powered by four 1,119 kW (1,500 hp) Wright GR-2600 Double Cyclone radial engines, the first flying-boat flew on 7 June 1938. It did not suffer from being underpowered, as had the XB-15 bomber, and all six were delivered to Pan American in the first half of 1939. Transatlantic mail services began on 20 May 1939, followed by the first passenger services on 29 June the same year, while others were used on the San Francisco-Hong Kong transpacific route.

Boeing Model 314A

The Model 314s proved entirely successful, and soon Pan American placed a follow-on order for six refined Model 314As, to be powered by 1,193 kW (1,600 hp) Double Cyclones. Fuel capacity was also increased by more than 25 per cent. The first Model 314A flew on 20 March 1941 and all had been delivered by July of the following year. Model 314s were brought up to this latest standard. Three of the Model 314As were resold by Pan American to BOAC, which used them on Atlantic and Empire communication routes.

With the United States then at war, the USAAF impressed one Model 314 and three Model 314As into military service as C-98 transports. After a short time the early aircraft was returned to Pan American but the Model 314As were transferred to the US Navy as utility transports, joining two other 314s. After the war they again joined Pan American, but the flying-boat era had passed and they were quickly retired.

Boeing Model 314 hull under construction

Right: **Boeing Model 314**

BOEING
Model 707-320C

USA

In the years ahead, when historians look back at the development of heavier-than-air craft during the 20th century, they will almost certainly regard Boeing's Model 707 as a classic creation of the aviation industry. Not only has it given valuable service in its originally intended role as a military tanker/transport, and in extensions to that military requirement, but built in very large numbers as a civil transport it has already, for more than a quarter of a century, proved to be one of the most valuable tools of the world's airlines. Itself a true giant in achievement, it set the pattern for a related family of civil airliners that now represent a significant total of the world's air transport vehicles.

Its development began in the early 1950s, when Boeing began as a private venture the design and construction of a demonstrator tanker/transport. It was intended that it would be able to provide inflight refuelling for existing and future jet bombers, fighters and reconnaissance aircraft, at or near their operational altitudes and speeds. Identified as the Model 367-80, the prototype (N70700) made its maiden flight on 15 July 1954: it was the first jet transport of US design and construction to be flown. Following successful demonstration to the USAF, it was announced in August 1954 that Boeing had been awarded a contract for the production of a tanker/transport version under the designation KC-135 Strato-tanker. Since that time they have been produced in large numbers, not only as tankers, but built or converted for a variety of special purposes, including the Boeing E-3 Sentry Airborne Warning and Control System (AWACS) aircraft.

Boeing Model 707-320C in Pacific Western Airlines livery

It would be naive to believe that, from the outset, Boeing had not intended to develop a civil transport from this same basic concept. The military contract would finance the original design and development and, subject to USAF approval, the company could proceed to build a civil version without undue delay. The approval came just less than a year following receipt of the military contract, on 13 July 1955, and the first 707-120 civil transport was flown for the first time on 20 December 1957.

Throughout the production life of the Model 707 there has been little change in basic configuration, other than the increased wing span and fuselage length given to the 707-320 Intercontinental to provide adequate payload/range capability for a true transoceanic role. This, in its 707-320C Convertible version, suitable for mixed passenger/cargo or all-cargo service, was the last of the civil line to be built when production ended in 1980. A cantilever low-wing monoplane of all-metal fail-safe construction, it incorporates swept wings and tail surfaces, has a retractable tricycle landing gear comprising a twin-wheel nose unit and four-wheel main bogies, and is powered by four fuel efficient 84.5 kN (19,000 lb st) Pratt & Whitney JT3D-7 turbofan engines mounted in pods beneath the wings. In a high density seating arrangement accommodation can be provided for a maximum of 219 passengers, and in an all-cargo configuration a maximum of 13 Type A containers can be loaded, a task simplified by a Boeing-developed cargo handling system installed on seven rows of seat tracks in the cabin floor. Cargo loading is via a 2.34 × 3.40 m (92 × 134 in) door incorporated in the forward fuselage on the port side.

Boeing 707s of all varieties remain in service with airlines and military users around the world. Despite the fact that the type first entered service in the late 1950s, this superb aeroplane is likely to be seen in our skies for many years to come.

BOEING
Model 747

USA

When details of Boeing's new Model 747 were first announced, on 13 April 1966, it was almost too much for the world's journalists. They soon discovered there was an inadequate supply of adjectives of magnitude. But one, quicker than the rest, coined the name Jumbo Jet. This soon entered the international vocabulary, and has remained in use by non-aviation people to describe this, the first of the world's wide-body jetliners. Understandably, a little time was needed to digest the announced statistics and implications of the 747. Paramount was a seating capacity that could total around 500 persons and, inevitably, there were those who could think only in terms of bigger and more horrific accidents. They, of course, were the negative thinkers but, clearly,

the introduction of such a large aircraft into worldwide service would create many problems. Just for starters there were those posed by embarking and disembarking an aircraft full of passengers and their baggage; of providing food and refreshment for them in flight; and of servicing these giants between arrival and departure in a minimum turnaround time. Would it prove possible to keep them flying sufficient hours each year to recoup their enormous capital cost? Would existing runways be suitable for their operation? The questions came quick and fast, but perhaps the happiest with the idea were the world's air traffic controllers. For them, aircraft of this class could offer some relief to a workload that was beginning to reach frightening proportions.

Boeing Model 747 during early flight trials, the world's first wide-body airliner

Right: **Boeing Model 747-200B operated by Philippine Airlines**

Like that visit to the dentist, many of the problems posed by imagination (and in this case by the media and ecologists) failed to materialise. The first of these aircraft flew on 9 February 1969, and the type entered service with remarkably little fuss on 22 January 1970, Pan-Am's New York-London service being used for the inaugural route. Since that time a number of versions have been built, with the 747-100B and 747-200B as the major passenger versions. The latter is available also as the -200B Combi and -200C Convertible for mixed passenger/cargo operations and -200F all-cargo Freighter. They are complemented by the short-range 747SR, long-range 747SP, and from 1983 an optional stretched upper deck will provide seating for a maximum of 69 passengers in an area that had been used originally as a passenger lounge. Under the US Air Force designation of E-4, the 747 has also been developed for use as an advanced Airborne Command Post to provide a vital communication link between the nation's high command and its strategic forces.

Boeing E-4B advanced airborne command post, based on the Model 747 and operated by the USAF Strategic Air Command

In configuration the basic 747 is a cantilever low-wing monoplane of all-metal fail-safe construction. The main cabin has an overall length of 57.00 m (187 ft), with a maximum width and height of 6.13 m (20 ft 1½ in) and 2.54 m (8 ft 4 in) respectively: two underfloor holds have a combined volume of 147 m³ (5,190 cu ft). When fully laden for take off, with 452 passengers on board, it can weigh as much as 377,840 kg (833,000 lb), which is almost 372 tons. To support the aircraft on the ground, and distribute this load over a large surface area, the tricycle landing gear incorporates a twinwheel nose unit, and four four-wheel main bogies. Not surprisingly, it needs a considerable amount of power for take-off and sustained flight, and this is provided by four turbofan engines, of General Electric, Pratt & Whitney, or Rolls-Royce manufacture, each giving an output of around 222.4 kN (50,000 lb st). To fuel them there is tankage for 198,385 litres (52,409 US gallons), sufficient to propel an average family car for something over one and a half million miles. With statistics like this, perhaps the 747 was aptly dubbed 'Jumbo Jet'.

The 'happy' transport – an Air France cargo-carrying version of the Model 747 with its hinged nose slightly raised and its side cargo door up

BOEING
XB-15

USA

Boeing's Model 294 was developed in strict secrecy over a three year period, designed to meet a USAAC specification of 1934 that called for a long-range heavy bomber. Designated XB-15, it was a mid-wing monoplane of all-metal construction except for the rear portions of the wings, which were covered with fabric. It had many innovations, including complete living accommodation for its crew and reserve crew, which included a flight engineer for the first time. Companionways through the huge wings provided access to the engines during flight. Power was to have been provided by four 1,492 kW (2,000 hp) Allison V-1710 engines, but, as these were not available in time, the bomber, originally designated XBLR-1 but later redesignated XB-15, received 634 kW (850 hp) Pratt & Whitney R-1830-11 Twin Wasp Sr radials.

Expected to carry four 0.30 in and two 0.50 in machine-guns for defence and a 3,629 kg (8,000 lb) bomb load, the XB-15 flew for the first time on 15 October 1937. From the start it became obvious that the Pratt & Whitney engines gave insufficient power to the huge aircraft, although it still managed to set several load-to-height records. But well before the bomber's first flight Boeing had already flown its smaller Model 299, which became the famed B-17 Flying Fortress, and it was this aircraft that entered production. Of course the XB-15 had been considered experimental from its conception, and so it is remembered mainly as having provided useful data that was later used in other projects that eventually led to the B-29 Superfortress.

As for the XB-15 itself, it was used as a military transport during the Second World War under the designation XC-105. Earlier, following an earthquake, it had been responsible for getting relief supplies into Chile from its base in Panama. It was scrapped in 1945.

Right: Boeing XB-15 bomber

Boeing XB-15 bomber

BORDELAISE
A.B.20 and D.B.71

France

Around 1931, the French company Société Aérienne Bordelaise, a member of the Société Générale Aéronautique and controlled by the Nieuport-Delage Company, had two new aircraft under test. One was a large 28-passenger strut-braced monoplane, known as the D.B.71, and the other was a military bomber derivative designated A.B.20.

Both aircraft were unusually configured, each with its thick-section monoplane wings attached

Bordelaise A.B.20

to the top longerons of two fuselages, and a very thick centre wing connecting the fuselages for part of their length. This arrangement allowed the D.B.71 to carry ten passengers in each fuselage and eight seated at tables in a large saloon in the centre wing. Power was provided by three 521 kW (700 hp) Lorraine Orion radial engines, one in the nose of each fuselage and one in the centre nose of the aircraft.

From the D.B.71 was developed the military A.B.20, which was basically similar in design but larger, was powered by four wing-mounted 447 kW (600 hp) Lorraine Courlis inline engines, and had a gun and bomb-aimer's position in the central nose. Two further gun positions were located in the rear of the thick centre wing, one above and one below. However, this bomber, like the D.B.71 airliner, did not progress beyond prototype stage.

BREGUET
521 Bizerte

France

In 1931 Breguet acquired a licence from the British firm of Short Brothers to construct the Short Calcutta flying-boat in France. After building a handful Breguet developed an enlarged version, which became the 521 Bizerte open-sea reconnaissance flying-boat for the French Navy and the 530 Saigon 20-passenger commercial type for Air Union

The prototype Bizerte flew for the first time on 11 September 1933. Its entire construction was of duralumin, except for the bottom of the hull and the stabilising floats, which were of stainless steel. Three 630 kW (845 hp) Gnome-Rhône 14Krsd radial engines were mounted in nacelles between the sesquiplane wings, driving three-blade metal propellers. Accommodation was provided for a bomb-aimer/gunner in the nose, in an open position. Behind this was an enclosed cockpit for two pilots side by side. To the rear were the wireless/navigation compartment, a two-berth cabin and toilet. The officers' quarters followed, with two bunks and a folding table, then a galley, workshop with fitter's bench, a mid-dorsal gunner's position and finally a tail-gunner's cockpit.

The Bizerte was ordered into production and thirty were built. These differed from the prototype mainly in armament, in having a long narrow glasshouse extension from the pilots' cockpit to the bow, and 14Kirs engines. Most of these served with 'Exploration' escadrilles of the French Aéronavale from 1935 until the end of the Second World War, latterly being used as maritime reconnaissance and anti-submarine aircraft. However, of the thirty, nine were captured by the Germans and were put to work between 1943 and 1945 for air-sea rescue.

As mentioned above, the commercial version was known as the Saigon, two of which had been ordered by Air Union. The first of these flew in 1934, by which time Air France had been formed from this airline and three others (later absorbing a fifth), in August 1933. It was therefore Air France that introduced the Saigon on trans-Mediterranean services in early 1935, each aircraft powered by three 585 kW (785 hp) Hispano-Suiza 12Ybr engines.

Breguet 521 Bizerte prototype

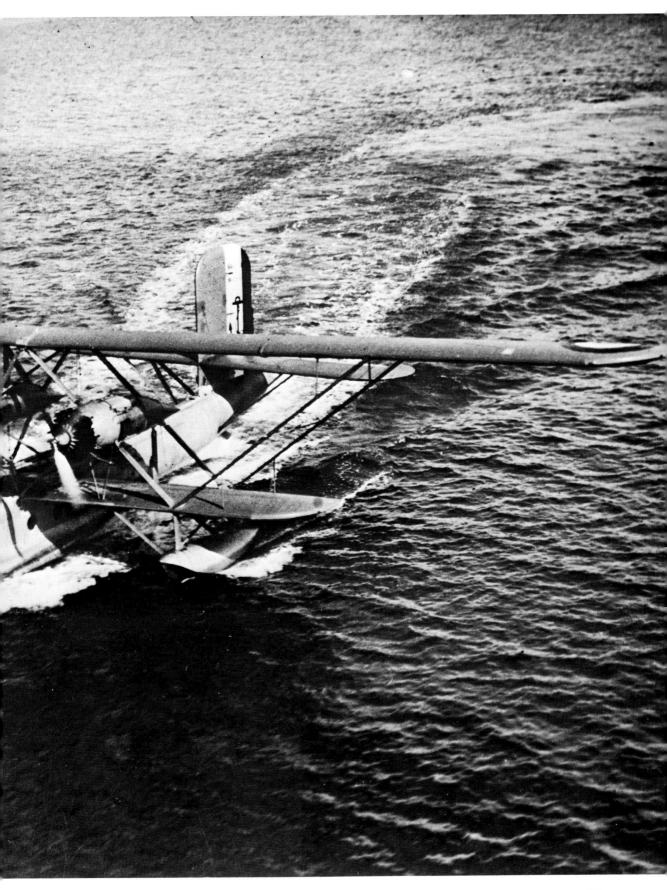

BREGUET
Type 763 Deux Ponts and Type 765 Sahara

France

In 1944 the design began of the Breguet Type 761 transport. The prototype, powered by four 1,193 kW (1,600 hp) SNECMA 14R engines, flew for the first time on 15 February 1949 and was awarded a certificate of airworthiness at an all-up weight of 40,000 kg (88,185 lb). It was followed by three pre-production aircraft known as Type 761Ss, the first of which flew in 1951. These were identical to the prototype except for their engines, which were 1,491 kW (2,000 hp) Pratt & Whitney R-2800 B31 radials. The Type 761S was awarded a C of A at an all-up weight of 45,000 kg (99,208 lb).

The first production version was the Type 763, a convertible passenger/cargo transport for Air France, with possible seating for 59 tourist passengers on the upper deck and 48 second-class passengers on the lower deck. The flight compartment was designed to meet Air France's request for the reduction of the flight crew from four to three. Power was provided by four 1,788 kW (2,400 hp) Pratt & Whitney R-2800 CA18 engines, driving Hamilton Standard reversing propellers.

Twelve were ordered in 1951, and the first of these flew on 20 July the same year. These were generally similar to the Type 761 but had reinforced wings of greater span. Known under the type name 'Provence' by Air France, the Type 763 entered service in March 1953 and operated between France and Algiers.

A military version of the airliner was the Type 765, powered by 1,790 kW (2,400 hp) R-2800 CB-16 or CB-17 engines. The easily-convertible accommodation on the two decks allowed for up to 126 fully-equipped troops, or 85 stretchers and medical attendants, or freight, vehicles and equipment, including a 14-ton tank. Loading and unloading of freight in the hold was through large rear panels beneath the fuselage, operated by hydraulic jacks, the lower deck floor being only 1.30 m (4 ft) from the ground to permit direct loading from trucks. Normal access for passengers was through lateral doors in the closed freight-loading panels, although another door was situated on the starboard side of the fuselage. Fifteen were ordered for the French Air Force in 1956, but this order was later cut to four. The first Type 765 flew on 6 September 1958.

Right: **Breguet Type 765 Sahara on display** (*Gordon S. Williams*)

Breguet Type 763 Deux Ponts (*Ministere des Armées 'Air'*)

BRISTOL
Brabazon

UK

An agreement was made between Britain and the USA during the Second World War to prevent duplication of effort by the aircraft industries of the two nations. And because the USA was involved in a war across the other side of the Pacific Ocean, it was logical for them to concentrate on the design and development of long-range transports. It was appreciated in Britain that in the long term this would give the Americans a head start in the production of civil airliners for post-war use. Accordingly, in early 1943, the government set up a committee, under the Chairmanship of Lord Brabazon, to make recommendations to manufacturers that would enable them to formulate designs while war was still in progress, assuming they had the necessary design capacity available.

First on the list of recommendations was the Type I, intended for transatlantic passenger services, and the Bristol Aeroplane Company was invited to proceed with the design of this aircraft. A small team was allocated to this task, and by November 1944 the company's Type 167 was beginning to take shape. In due course, and appropriately, it became known as the Brabazon, with work on construction of the first of two prototypes beginning in 1945.

A cantilever low-wing monoplane of all-metal construction, with a slender circular-section pressurised fuselage, it had a conventional tail unit incorporating a very tall fin and rudder. The retractable tricycle landing gear had a twinwheel nose unit, with each main unit consisting of two twin-tyred wheels. Power was provided by eight 1,842 kW (2,470 hp) Bristol Centaurus radial engines, mounted within the wing, each pair driving two counter-rotating propellers on a coaxial shaft. This meant that each propeller was driven by its own engine. The first prototype had no passenger accommodation as first flown, carrying within the cabin area an extensive array of instrumentation and data-recording equipment.

The first flight of the Brabazon I (G-AGPW) was made by the company's chief test pilot, A.J. Pegg, on 4 September 1949. The maiden flight, and those which followed, revealed no handling problems of this, the largest landplane built and flown in the UK. It was not until some four months later that a hydraulic failure made it necessary to land at Filton without the use of trailing-edge flaps, but this was achieved successfully by the use of propeller reversal to minimise the higher speed of touchdown.

The Brabazon was flown subsequently with 30 seats in the rear fuselage, making it possible for officials from various airlines and government departments to gain an appreciation of the

Bristol Brabazon under construction in January 1948

Bristol Brabazon roll-out

Below: **Bristol Brabazon**

excellent cabin environment of what was then considered to be a very big aeroplane. But, although BEA wanted to use it between London and Nice, France, development came to an end following an indication of fatigue problems. As a result, the second prototype, which was to have been equipped to carry 100 passengers, and be powered by turboprop engines, was never completed. Those who are old enough to have seen the mighty Brabazon in flight will remember it with pride.

CAMERON BALLOONS A.530

UK

Starting in a small way as a manufacturer of hot-air balloons in 1968, Cameron Balloons, based at Bristol, England, has since become one of the giants of this popular and growing industry. Popular, because in an age of noise and turmoil there is something both soothing and satisfying in just 'floating on the breeze': growing, because of the foregoing comment, plus the fact that it has proved to be a comparatively cheap way of experiencing flight for pleasure.

Inevitably, this lighter-than-air vehicle was soon involved in a new area of record attempts, and in early 1981 hot-air balloons manufactured by the Cameron company held the world's absolute distance record of 674.53 km (419.13 miles); absolute duration record of 24 hours, 7 minutes, 58 seconds; and, subject to confirmation by the FAI, an absolute altitude record of 17,404 m (57,100 ft). To add to these giant achievements, the company built the world's largest hot-air balloon, the *Gerard A. Heineken*, with a volume of 14,158 m (500,000 cu ft), and also built and flew the world's first hot-air airship. To complete the Cameron record of achievement, it should be mentioned that during 1978 Don Cameron, and Major Christopher Davey, in the combined helium/hot-air balloon *Zanussi*, were beaten by a distance of only 161 km (100 miles) from becoming the first balloonists to cross the North Atlantic. The company was, in late 1981, continuing the development of an advanced balloon of this type with which it is intended to attempt a round-the-world flight.

The foregoing leaves few giant achievements for the company to attain, yet it has managed more. During 1981 the company has completed construction of a new hot-air balloon, designated as the Cameron A.530 and which, with a capacity of 15,000 m³ (530,000 cu ft), is currently the world's largest hot-air balloon. Designed and built for record-breaking purposes, under the sponsorship of Hennessy Brandy and Kodachrome, this new balloon has a basket that accommodates only two people. This comparatively small basket is, however, designed to support a quantity of gas cylinders, and is topped by a burner with one main and four auxiliary jets. The combination of this burner and the volume of the envelope, provides a total lift of approximately 5,080 kg (11,200 lb), sufficient to airlift about 33 passengers in a suitably designed basket. Other giant-sized statistics of the A.530's envelope, which has 20 gores, each built up from 42 horizontal panels, include some 3,000 m² (32,290 sq ft) of fabric used in its construction, plus 90 m² (969 sq ft) of flame-resistant Nomex fabric, 950 m (3,117 ft) of load tapes, 700 m (2,297 ft) of other tapes, and a total envelope weight of 268 kg (590 lb). The control of such a huge vehicle has called for special attention from the designers. A controllable curtain system, within the crown of the envelope, and which can be opened and reclosed, allows for lift-dumping, and there is also a circular ripping system which, when the vehicle is on the ground, is used to spill all hot air from the envelope. Even this could be inadequate when a landing is made in gusting or strong winds, and an emergency system allows for the envelope to be detached from the basket immediately it touches the ground. A cord attached to the crown of the envelope inverts it as it rises in the air: five slits in the lower panels then allow the envelope to separate, 'like a peeled banana', allowing the enclosed ball of hot air to disperse immediately.

First flown in Britain on 1 May 1981, the A.530 (G-BIWM; constructor's number 701) was then transferred to its base in France. From there it was taken to Ballina, West Eire, for an attempt on the world distance record. On 25 November 1981, crewed by Michel Arnould and Hélène Dorigny, it lifted off from there at 01.32 hrs BST, landing at St. Christophe-en-Boucherie, France at 06.37 hrs on 26 November. In the course of the 29 hr 5 min flight a distance of 1,153 km (716.4 miles) had been covered and, subject to ratification by the FAI, represents new world endurance and distance records for a hot-air balloon. Strangely enough, the landing site was little more than 160 km (100 miles) from Annonay, where the whole business of hot air ballooning first began.

The Cameron Balloons' A.530 *Semiramis*

58

CAPRONI
Ca 90P.B

Italy

During the First World War Italy had launched the first sustained strategic bombing offensive ever, against Austria-Hungary from 20 August 1915. The main types of bomber used during the early stages were the Caproni Ca2 and 3, both 22.20 m (72 ft 10 in)-span biplanes, powered by three engines. The Ca 2 bomber undertook the first Italian night bombing raids. Before the Armistice Caproni produced other large bombers, including the massive Ca 4 triplane with a wing span of 29.9 m (98 ft 1 in).

In 1923, when Benito Mussolini formed the Regia Aeronautica, the heavy bomber force had to rely for a time on the Ca 3. However, in 1925 Caproni flew the prototype Ca 73, a 25 m (82 ft)-span bomber with inverted sesquiplane wings and powered by two engines in tandem. The general layout of the Ca 73, which became a standard Italian bomber, was used again and again by Caproni in later designs, including the Ca 90P.B.

Appearing in 1929, the Ca 90P.B was then the largest bomber in the world. Its six 746 kW (1,000 hp) Isotta-Fraschini Asso engines were arranged in tandem pairs, one pair carried above the fuselage midway between the wings and the other pairs built into the extremities of the bottom wing centre-section. The wings, fuselage and tail unit were steel tube structures, fabric covered, and accommodation was provided for a gunner in the nose of the fuselage, two pilots ahead of the lower wing leading-edge, a gunner to the rear of the wings with machine-guns above, below and in the sides of the fuselage, and lastly a gunner in the centre of the upper wing. The main bomb compartment was under the wings in the fuselage, capable of packing 8,000 kg (17,637 lb) of bombs. Unfortunately for Caproni, this bomber was not put into production, but in February 1930 it did manage to set up six world records carrying payloads of 5,000, 7,500 and 10,000 kg.

Right: Caproni Ca 90P.B

Caproni Ca 42 triplane (Ca 4 sub-variant), one of Italy's giant strategic bombers operated during the First World War

CAPRONI
Ca 60 Triple Hydro-Triplane

Italy

As noted in the previous entry, Caproni developed several large bombers during 1915-18. Although in 1923 the wartime Ca 3 re-entered production for the air force, immediately after the Armistice Caproni concentrated on the development of mainly commercial aircraft. Without doubt the strangest was the Triple Hydro-Triplane, an enormous flying-boat intended only as an oversized model with which to obtain reliable data as to the efficiency of multi-planes in juxtaposition, from which a much larger transatlantic flying-boat could be designed.

Powered by eight 298 kW (400 hp) Liberty engines at the extreme ends, the Triple Hydro-Triplane embodied the latest Italian ideas on tailless and elevatorless multi-engined aircraft. As completed, the only surfaces which could act as elevators were small vanes located between the hull and the floats and were intended to assist the hull in leaving the water. The hull itself was arranged to accommodate up to 100 passengers,

Caproni Triple Hydro-Triplane

7,700 kg (17,000 lb) of mail and cargo, or, in military guise, eight torpedoes and eight bombs, distributed over the length of the machine. Consequently, the longitudinal moment of inertia of the aircraft was enormous. But the distribution of load was such that all three sets of triple wings had to be virtually equally loaded, with longitudinal control apparently supplied by opposed use of the ailerons of the rear and front planes. As a result, the Triple Hydro-Triplane was not merely unstable but also virtually uncontrollable longitudinally. An interesting feature of the design was the ability of the pilot to stop or start any engine in flight by signalling electrically to the mechanics in charge of the five forward engines (two tandem pairs and a central tractor-mounted engine) and the three aft engines (two tractor-mounted and one pusher).

The Triple Hydro-Triplane began taxying trials on Lake Maggiore towards the end of February 1921. On 2 March a straight flight of about 1.6 km (1 mile) was made. Two days later the flying-boat was again readied for a flight. Having taken off, it appears from contemporary reports that the Triple Hydro-Triplane made a determined and uncheckable slow descent into the water, causing considerable damage to the hull. Thereafter the flying-boat was abandoned.

CIERVA
W.11 Air Horse

UK

Designed originally to provide a crop-dusting/spraying helicopter for use by Pest Control Ltd, the large W.11 developed by the Cierva company was essentially a three-rotor experimental helicopter. The complications of producing a three-rotor/single-engined layout was forced upon the company by the fact that a gross weight of some 8,165 kg (18,000 lb) was called for. Within the contemporary state of rotary-wing art, engineering and practical learning imposed an effective limit on a rotor diameter of about 15.24 m (50 ft), and calculations showed that three rotors of this size would be needed. As a result, the entire structure was dominated by the rotors and their support structure and, strange to believe, the

Cierva W.11 Air Horse

forward support struts of the front rotor were directly in the pilot's field of view.

In overall configuration the three rotors, viewed in plan, had their rotor heads at the apices of an equilateral triangle (i.e. with a separation of 120 degrees). All three rotated in the same direction and, to overcome the effects of torque, their planes of rotation were slightly tilted. They were carried on a triangulated outrigger structure, which served also to support the main units of the tricycle landing gear. Heavy main frames were incorporated in the all-metal rectangular-section fuselage structure to provide mounting points for the outrigger struts and bracing. An all-metal cantilever tail unit consisted of a horizontal surface, mounting all-moving fins at the tips. The single engine, a 1,208 kW (1,620 hp) supercharged Rolls-Royce Merlin 24, was mounted in a compartment within the aft fuselage, driving the rotors through a distributor gearbox.

The pilot and co-pilot, seated side by side, were accommodated in a flight deck in the fuselage nose. Behind them was a large compartment,

Cierva W.11 Air Horse (*Flight*)

5.79 m (19 ft) in length, which would have been used to contain chemical tanks and dispersal equipment for the agricultural role. However, it was appreciated that it would also be possible to utilise the Air Horse in passenger and cargo roles, with accommodation for up to 24 passengers or some 1,678 kg (3,700 lb) of cargo respectively, and accordingly the aft fuselage was completed with clamshell doors that could be opened to allow direct loading or unloading of bulky items.

During the evolution of the W.11 design, negotiations between Saunders-Roe Ltd and the Cierva company had resulted in formation of the Saunders-Roe Helicopter Division. It was planned by the latter that Cunliffe-Owen would build the structures of two prototypes, but when this company closed shortly afterwards, Saunders-Roe assumed responsibility for their construction. The first of these (G-ALCV), was first seen in the static exhibition at the 1948 SBAC Show, its maiden flight being made on 7 December 1948 at Eastleigh, Hampshire. It represented an important event for British aviation, for it was then the largest single-engined helicopter in the world. Development flying continued, but on 13 June 1950 the Air Horse crashed, due to the failure of a rotor hub, and all on board were killed. The second prototype (G-ALCW) was completed and flown in tethered form, but the project was abandoned when this, too, suffered rotor failure.

CONSOLIDATED
B-32 Dominator

USA

The USAAF's requirement of early 1940 for a 'Hemisphere Defense Weapon' was to result in the receipt of submissions from Boeing, Consolidated, Douglas, and Lockheed. Allocated the respective designations XB-29, XB-32, XB-31, and XB-30, the last two failed to survive the design development stage, and prototypes of Boeing's proposal, built as the B-29 Superfortress (q.v.), and the Consolidated XB-32 were ordered by the Army Air Force.

Designed to meet the same advanced specification as the B-29, the Consolidated XB-32 was also intended to have the same complications of pressurised compartments for the crew, and remotely operated weapons. The main difference between the two types was that Boeing solved the problems posed by these two features, with the result that B-29s were first used operationally in June 1944. Consolidated failed, abandoning pressurisation and remote-control gun turrets. The delays occasioned by the attempts to overcome these development snags were extensive, and only fifteen production B-32s saw limited action in the Western Pacific during the closing stages of the Second World War.

In configuration the B-32, named Dominator, had a high-set cantilever monoplane wing. This was very similar to that of the company's B-24 Liberator, being a Davis high aspect ratio wing for which Consolidated had acquired the patent rights. The wing had good lift characteristics, which meant that it could be set at a lower-drag angle of attack, giving extended range capability. Because the aircraft was intended to be pressurised a circular-section fuselage had been chosen, and though flown initially with a twin tail unit similar to that of the B-24, it acquired a conventional unit with a very tall fin and rudder in its production form. The retractable tricycle landing gear had twin wheels on each unit. Power was provided by four 1,715 kW (2,300 hp) Wright R-3350-23 Duplex Cyclone radial engines, mounted in wing leading-edge nacelles, and driving four-blade reversible-pitch propellers. Accommodation was provided for a crew of eight, including five gunners in nose, tail, ventral, and two dorsal turrets, each gunner having two 0.50 in machine-guns. A maximum bombload of 9,072 kg (20,000 lb) could be carried in tandem fuselage bays.

The three prototypes were flown on 7 September 1942, 2 July and 9 November 1943, but it was not until almost the end of 1944 that the first production aircraft was delivered. Orders totalled 1,588, but only 115 had been built when war-end contract cancellations terminated production. Of this total, 40 were converted into TB-32 trainers.

Consolidated B-32 Dominator on the Yontan airstrip in August 1945 (*US Air Force*)

CONSOLIDATED
PB2Y Coronado

Consolidated PB2Y-3 Coronado transport, with gun turrets removed

USA

The prototype of the Consolidated P3Y-1 patrol flying-boat had been flown for the first time at the end of March 1935. Early flight testing showed that it was an outstanding aircraft, and the manufacturer was rewarded by an initial order for 60 for the US Navy. With the award of this contract, the designation was changed from P (patrol) to PB (patrol bomber), signifying that the type was able to carry a substantial bombload. The aircraft became known as the PBY-5 Catalina, one of the most successful flying-boats of the Second World War. Although delighted with early evaluation of the XP3Y-1, the Navy was soon making plans for the development of a larger

four-engined flying-boat patrol bomber. After evaluating proposals from both Sikorsky and Consolidated, a prototype of Sikorsky's design was ordered under the designation XPBS-1 in late June 1935, followed by a Consolidated flying-boat as the XPB2Y-1 in July 1936. Following evaluation of these two prototypes, the XPB2Y-1 was considered to be the most suitable. In March 1939 Consolidated received an initial order for six PB2Y-2s.

The PB2Ys were of all-metal construction, having a broad and deep hull to accommodate a crew of ten and a 5,443 kg (12,000 lb) bombload. Its high-set cantilever monoplane wing incor-

Consolidated PB2Y-2 Coronado

porated retractable wingtip stabilising floats, and also mounted the power plant of four Pratt & Whitney R-1830-78 radials in leading-edge nacelles, each with a two-stage supercharger. The prototype had been flown initially with a single fin and rudder, but in its final form had a high-mounted tailplane with two elevators and carrying large endplate fins and rudders. This layout was adopted for the production aircraft. Defensive armament comprised six 0.50-in machine-guns in bow, dorsal, and tail turrets. The first of these production aircraft entered service with the Navy on the last day of 1940, by which time an improved PB2Y-3, with 895 kW (1,200 hp)

R-1830-88 engines had been ordered. This represented the most extensively built version (210), and other improvements included the installation of self-sealing fuel tanks and the addition of two more machine-guns in beam positions. An unspecified number carried ASV radar.

The type, named Coronado by the RAF (which received 10 for use as transports), saw little operational service with the US Navy. The RAF's PB2Y-3Bs were used for transatlantic freight and passenger services, and the USN subsequently converted 31 for a transport role under the designation PB2Y-3R. Other variants included PB2Y-5s and PB2Y-5Rs, these given R-1830-92 engines, which offered better performance at low altitude; and a number of other -3 conversions produced the PB2Y-5H for casualty evacuation. Equipped to carry 25 stretchers, these latter aircraft were to give valuable service in the Pacific theatre of operations.

CONSOLIDATED VULTEE
B-36

USA

Derived from the amalgamation of Consolidated Aircraft and Vultee Aircraft during 1943, Consolidated Vultee was, at the end of the Second World War, America's largest aircraft manufacturer. It was appropriate, therefore, that this company should produce the biggest bomber to enter service with the nation's air force, with

Below: Convair XB-36 prototype with single main landing gear wheels and original style of nose

Bottom: Convair B-36 (*US Air Force*)

initial production delivery of B-36As made to the USAAF towards the end of August 1947, only about three weeks before establishment of the independent US Air Force.

The specification that led to creation of this giant had been drawn up in early 1941, before America became directly involved in the war. It was based on a possibility that, in the event of a successful invasion of Britain by German forces, it might prove essential for the USAAF to bomb European targets from bases in the USA. Such a capability needed a range of some 8,050 km (5,000 miles) with a 4,536 kg (10,000 lb) bombload, and a return to base without any intermediate refuelling. The realisation of such an aircraft took considerable time.

Convair B-36D bombers and RB-36 strategic reconnaissance aircraft under construction at Fort Worth

Following circulation of the requirement to US manufacturers, and the study of submissions, Consolidated Aircraft received a contract for two XB-36 prototypes during 1941. However, development proceeded at a low key, and it was not until Japan's forces were established over vast areas of the Pacific that possible use of the B-36 in that theatre added new urgency. In the event, it was not until some eleven months after Japan's surrender that the XB-36 prototype flew for the first time, on 8 August 1946.

The big requirement led to a big aeroplane with slightly swept wings. Its fuselage contained two pressurised crew compartments, joined by a 24.38 m (80 ft) long tunnel which was traversed on a wheeled trolley. The tail unit was conventional, and the retractable tricycle landing gear incorporated twin nosewheels, with a four-wheel bogie on each main unit. Power for the first B-36A production version comprised six 2,237 kW (3,000 hp) Pratt & Whitney R-4360-25 radials, these installed near the wing trailing-edge to drive three-blade constant-speed fully-feathering and reversible pusher propellers. The B-36A was basically a training and familiarisation version, carrying no armament.

It was followed by the B-36B, equipped for operational use, and with armament comprising sixteen 20 mm cannon, mounted in six retractable remotely-controlled turrets, and in nose and tail positions. Subsequent versions and conversions included the B-36D, which supplemented the six piston engines with four General Electric J47-GE-19 turbojets, each of 23.1 kN (5,200 lb st), paired in pods beneath each wing. With such power it was possible to carry two massive Grand Slam bombs. RB-36D reconnaissance aircraft carried 14 cameras and a crew of 22; and the designation RB-36E applied to generally similar aircraft resulting from conversions. B-36Fs had 2,834 kW (3,800 hp) R-4360-53 radials, and the similar RB-36F had increased fuel capacity. Final production versions were the B-36H, RB-36H, and B-36J with detail improvements.

Perhaps the strangest of these aircraft were some dozen GRB-36Fs equipped to carry, deploy and recover Republic GRF-84Fs, which could make high-speed reconnaissance penetrations of vital targets, returning to the mother aircraft for the long-range return to base. The sheer size of these aircraft suggested they would be suitable for the installation of nuclear power plant. One NB-36H carried a nuclear reactor for test purposes, but this was for the evaluation of shielding and possible effects on instrumentation: plans to build a nuclear-powered version failed to materialise. The designation YB-36G was applied to a project for a B-36 with all-turbojet power plant, and resulting in two YB-60 prototypes that had more acutely swept wings and eight Pratt & Whitney J57 turbojets. No production examples were built.

Convair GRB-36F, an RB-36 strategic reconnaissance aircraft modified to carry a Republic GRF-84F Thunderflash reconnaissance plane in 'parasite' fashion to extend range and enhance survivability

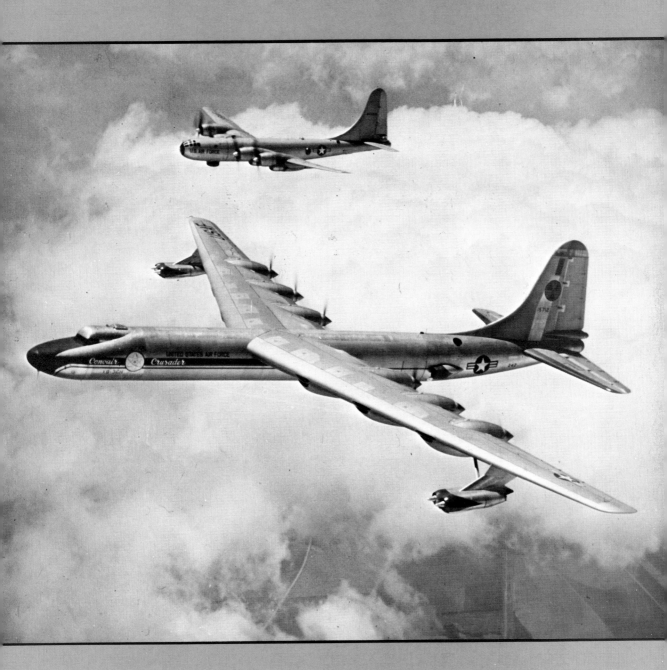

Convair NB-36H Crusader, based on the B-36, was the first
aeroplane to carry a nuclear reactor

CONSOLIDATED
XC-99

USA

Involvement in the Pacific theatre of operations, following Japan's attack on Pearl Harbor, was made doubly difficult by the serious losses of naval power that were suffered in that attack. While it might have seemed that this was but a temporary situation, the air superiority held by the Japanese for some time after this opening gambit resulted in further serious losses for Allied seapower in the Pacific. It represented a particularly difficult problem, for with the Japanese holding the initiative, both on the sea and in the air, it seemed extremely hazardous to introduce into the area desperately needed shipping. Without the supply by sea of reinforcements, supplies and weapons, the situation could not be reversed. History relates the solutions, but this situation was to lead to the development of a new generation of transport aircraft, able to bring in men and/or logistics, or to evacuate casualties, even though the battle zone and home base were separated by some thousands of overwater miles.

This line of thought led to the development of a number of superb transports, stemming from civil airliners or military bomber designs that were in the pipeline during 1941. In addition, prototypes were built of a small number of subsequent designs that clearly had some potential for use in this kind of role. One of these derived from the Consolidated B-36 bomber (q.v.), with a single prototype ordered under the designation XC-99 on 31 December 1942.

The XC-99 retained the wings, tail unit, landing gear and power plant of the B-36B, but introduced a completely new fuselage. This was considerably deeper than that of the bomber version, making it possible to include two decks that were able to accommodate a maximum of 400 fully-equipped troops. The upper deck (including the flight deck) was 48.16 m (158 ft) in length, with two staircases that connected with lower forward and rear decks that were separated by the wing structure. For casualty evacuation, up to 300 stretchers could be carried or, alternatively, 45,359 kg (100,000 lb) of freight. Electric hoists on overhead rollers extended the length of both cargo areas, and electrically-actuated cargo hatches in the lower fuselage could be opened in flight to allow air dropping of cargo and supplies.

The XC-99 was operated by a crew of five, and there was accommodation for a relief crew to be carried for long-distance missions.

First flown on 23 November 1947, extensive company testing was carried out before the aircraft was handed over to the USAF on 26 May 1949. Based at Kelly AFB, it was used for special transcontinental cargo missions, and on one occasion airlifted a maximum load exceeding 45,813 kg (101,000 lb). Before being retired from service in 1957, this one and only XC-99 had established a number of unofficial distance/payload records, including the carriage of 38,555 kg (85,000 lb) of cargo over a range of 3,701 km (2,300 miles).

Right: Consolidated XC-99, then the world's largest landplane

Consolidated XC-99

CONVAIR
R3Y Tradewind

USA

Under the designation XP5Y-1, the US Navy ordered two prototypes of a large patrol flying-boat, the first of these making its maiden flight on 18 April 1950. Unique as the only turboprop-powered flying-boat to serve with the Navy, the type was also readily distinguishable by its unusual hull configuration. A product of Convair's Hydrodynamic Research Laboratory at San Diego, this had a length-to-beam ratio of 10 to 1, which was double that of previous flying-boats built by the company. Other features of this aircraft's configuration included a high-set cantilever wing, carrying strut-mounted stabilising floats beneath the outer panels and mounting the four 4,101 ekW (5,500 ehp) Allison XT-40A-4 engines in nacelles at the leading-edges. The hull terminated in an upswept section, mounting the tail unit, and the accommodation was both pressurised and air-conditioned.

Development of the type by the company was somewhat protracted, and it was not until 23 February 1954 that the first production R3Y-1 Tradewind was flown. The changed designation, without the inclusion of the letter P, shows that the Navy had by then decided to use the type for transport rather than patrol. Thus, the five

Convair R3Y Tradewind unloading a tractor and gun

production R3Y-1s were all equipped for operation in personnel or cargo-carrying roles, or could be used alternatively as air ambulances. Each was operated normally by a crew of five, and when used as a personnel transport, all passenger seats were rear-facing. Access doors for passengers were provided on each side of the hull, and a 3.05 m (10 ft) wide door was incorporated in the port side of the hull, just aft of the wings, to facilitate cargo loading.

Production was completed by the construction of six generally similar R3Y-2s. They differed by having more powerful T40-A-10 turboprops, each developing 4,362 ekW (5,850 ehp), and by being configured especially for a heavy transport

Convair R3Y Tradewind

role. As a result, the nose of the hull could swing upwards to allow direct in-loading of vehicles from a beach or quay, via a built-in folding ramp. The flight deck had been raised somewhat to ensure that it caused no restriction to the loading of vehicles. As an alternative to heavy vehicles, the cabin could be equipped with 80 easily removable rear-facing seats for personnel, or could be equipped to operate in a casualty-evacuation role, carrying up to 72 stretchers and 12 medical attendants. These two types entered service with the US Navy's Fleet Logistic Wings, Pacific, during 1956. At a later date, the R3Y-2 Tradewinds were converted for use as four-point flight refuelling tankers, equipped with the probe-and-drogue system developed by the British company, Flight Refuelling Ltd.

DORNIER
Do X

Germany

The Do X was the largest flying-boat built up to the Second World War, although in design it was surpassed by other giants such as the Short Sarafand. Because of the restrictions in aircraft production imposed by the Treaty of Versailles, it was built at Altenrhein in Switzerland by Aktiengesellschaft für Dornier-Flugzeugwerke, and flew for the first time on 25 July 1929.

In every aspect the Do X was big. Its high-mounted strut-braced wing had a span of 48 m (157 ft 5 in) and was a metal structure, with corrugated light alloy and fabric covering. Power was originally provided by no less than twelve Siemens-built Bristol Jupiter radial engines, but these were eventually replaced by a similar number of 447 kW (600 hp) Curtiss Conquerors. The huge two-step hull was of typical Dornier type, using a sharp knife-bow with a concavely curved bottom to the first step, then a V-shaped bottom to the hull with a lessening included angle up to the rear step, where a water-rudder was fitted. At the front step were the 'Dornier-Stummel' or sponsons, which gave lateral stability in the water. These also served as part of the wing-bracing structure. The two pilots sat side-by-side in a totally enclosed deckhouse forward of the wing, behind which was the captain's cabin and navigation room, then the engineers' compartment and wireless compartment. Below were the passenger compartments, which accommodated up to 150 people. However, on 21 October 1929 the Do X lifted off with 150 passengers, a crew of ten and nine stowaways!

The Do X's most notable flight was from Friedrichshafen to New York, beginning on 2 November 1930 and ending on 27 August 1931. It flew via Amsterdam, Calshot (England), Lisbon (where the wing was damaged by fire), Canary Islands (where the hull was damaged), Bolama (Portuguese Guinea), Cape Verde Islands, Fernando Noronha, Natal (Brazil), Rio de Janeiro and the West Indies. Two other New York flights were made, as well as one to South America and other journeys, but the design was quite impracticable and so was commercially doomed. However, two sister Do Xs were built for Italy, named *Umberto Maddalena* and *Alessandro Guidoni*, but these were equally unsuccessful and were passed to the military for a short time.

Dornier Do X, the largest flying-boat of the inter-war period
Right: **Dornier Do X**

Rear view of the Dornier Do X with the original Jupiter radial engines

Below: Interior of a Dornier Do X

DOUGLAS
C-124 Globemaster II

USA

Design and development of the Douglas C-74 Globemaster I transport began during the Second World War, but contract cancellations that came after VJ-Day were to result in the production of only 14 for the USAAF. Intended for use as a long-range heavy transport, it was found to have exceptional load-carrying capability, and following discussions between Douglas and the then renamed USAF, it was decided to use a C-74 airframe as the basis for a new heavy strategic cargo transport.

Development of the design was to result in the YC-124 prototype, which retained the low-set cantilever monoplane wings of the C-74, its conventional tail unit, and 2,610 kW (3,500 hp) Pratt & Whitney R-4360-49 Wasp Major radial engines, installed in wing leading-edge nacelles. Many other proven components of the C-74 were used in this prototype, but basically it added the above assemblies to a complete new fuselage and more robust retractable tricycle landing gear. The new deep fuselage was of rectangular cross-section, some 4.27 m (14 ft) in width, with provision for conversion to a double deck cabin when used as a troop transport. Its large rounded nose incorporated clamshell doors, providing an opening 3.56 m (11 ft 8 in) high and 3.45 m (11 ft 4 in) wide through which tracked or wheeled vehicles could be driven or hauled up built-in ramps. Two overhead travelling cranes, each with a maximum capacity of 7,257 kg (16,000 lb), ran above the full length of the 23.47 m (77 ft) long

Douglas C-124C Globemaster II

hold. An unusual loading feature, developed originally for the C-74, comprised an electrically-actuated cargo lift in the floor of the hold, just aft of the wing trailing-edges. The flight deck was high in the nose, above the clamshell doors, and accommodation was provided for a crew of five. If used in a transport role, with two decks installed, a maximum of 200 fully-equipped troops could be carried, or 123 stretcher cases, 45 ambulatory patients, and 15 medical attendants.

First flown on 27 November 1949, the development programme of the YC-124 progressed smoothly, and leading to an order for a pre-production prototype and 28 C-124As, allocated the name Globemaster II. Apart from having similarly-powered R-4360-20WA engines and detail changes in equipment, they were identical to the original prototype, and a total of 204 C-124As was to be built. Some were modified subsequently by the addition of weather radar, plus the installation of combustion heaters in wingtip pods to provide wing and tail de-icing and cabin heating.

The second production version, the C-124C (243 built), had the radar and combustion heaters as standard, increased fuel capacity, and more powerful R-4360-63A engines, each developing 2,834 kW (3,800 hp) and allowing operation at higher gross weights. A single YC-124B prototype was built with 4,101 ekW (5,500 ehp) Pratt & Whitney YT34-P-6 turboprop engines. This had started life as a flight refuelling tanker project designated YKC-124B. When this failed to gain USAF support, the YC-124B continued to serve as an engine testbed. In conjunction with the C-133 Cargomaster (q.v.), Globemaster IIs remained in service until the C-5A Galaxy (q.v.) became operational in 1970.

Loading a bus through the nose-doors of a Douglas C-124A Globemaster II

Right: **Douglas C-124A Globemaster II**

DOUGLAS
C-133 Cargomaster

USA

US Army Air Force involvement in the Second World War, in which the nation had been fighting in military theatres that were separated from the homeland by major oceans, had emphasised the military importance of strategic transport aircraft. Early post-war events, such as the Berlin Airlift and war in Korea, merely stressed how essential such aircraft could be if conflicts were to be controlled before they got out of hand.

In the early 1950s, the Douglas Aircraft Company received development contracts from the USAF for two large turboprop-powered strategic transport aircraft. The first of these had the designation C-132, but failed to materialise, and was cancelled in 1956. Had it been built, the intended wing span of 56.90 m (186 ft 8 in) and maximum take-off weight of almost 213,200 kg

(470,000 lb) in a tanker configuration, would almost certainly have guaranteed its inclusion in this book. However, it is the smaller of the two, the C-133, that survived to be built in small numbers.

Detail design of this transport, to meet the requirements of the USAF's Logistic Carrier Supporting System SS402L, began in early 1953. No prototype was built, and the first C-133A was flown for the first time on 23 April 1956. It was seen to be of cantilever high-wing monoplane configuration, its large circular-section fuselage pressurised, heated and ventilated, and providing a cargo compartment 27.43 m (90 ft) in length. This was loaded via a two-section rear door, the lower section forming a ramp that could support a load of 11,340 kg (25,000 lb), and making it possible for vehicles up to 3.66 m (12 ft) in height to be driven straight into the cargo hold. A large forward side door allowed direct loading of

Douglas C-133 Cargomaster

freight from a truck or trailer. At that time, the dimensions of the ramp and cargo hold were such that the Cargomaster could accept almost every type of vehicle used by the US Army. To ensure that the hold was not in any way obstructed, two large external pods, one on each side of the fuselage, provided housings for the four-wheel main landing gear units when retracted, that on the port side also accommodating dual auxiliary power units to cater for the pressurisation and ventilation requirements.

The first of the C-133As for the USAF's Military Air Transport Service were delivered in August 1957, these being powered by four wing-mounted Pratt & Whitney T34-P-3 turboprops, each developing 4,482 ekW (6,000 eshp). Late production C-133As had T34-P-7W engines with water-injection, giving each a maximum power rating of 5,294 ekW (7,100 eshp). The last three of 35 C-133As were provided with clamshell rear

loading doors, adding 0.91 m (3 ft) to the length of the cargo hold, and making it possible for these particular C-133As to carry Titan missiles without disassembly.

Production terminated in 1961 after an additional 15 C-133Bs had been built. These differed by having more powerful T34-P-9W turboprops, each developing 5,593 ekW (7,500 eshp), and also incorporated the clamshell rear loading doors that had been introduced on the last three C-133As. This fleet of 50 aircraft was to see extensive use, particularly during operations in Viet-Nam, but were retired in 1971 when fatigue problems made it desirable to withdraw them from service. An attempt was made in 1973, by a non-profit making organisation, to convert four of the stored C-133As for use as flying hospitals. It was intended that they should be kept available to fly to any point in the world where a major disaster had occurred. However, this excellent intention proved unsuccessful because, as a result of the fatigue problem, the US Federal Aviation Administration was unprepared to grant any form of type certificate for their operation.

Douglas C-133 Cargomaster and C-124 Globemaster II transports in Viet-Nam during 1964 (*US Air Force*)

DOUGLAS
XB-19

USA

In the mid-1930s, far-seeing members of the General Staff of the US Army Air Corps were forced into a difficult situation. Because of the nation's isolationist policy, strengthened by earlier involvement in the First World War, it had become virtually impossible to procure new aircraft other than for the nation's defence. The perpetuation of such a policy would mean that if the US became involved in a modern, fast-moving war, there would be inadequate time to develop and manufacture the weapons it would need. Thus, the strategic bombers required to attack an enemy's industrial resources had to be procured by clandestine means, under the guise of defence weapons.

It began with Project A, under which one prototype XBLR-1 (experimental bomber long-range) was contracted from Boeing in July 1935. Later designated XB-15, this large and impressive bomber was low on performance, but experience gained in its construction was to prove valuable in development of the B-17 Flying Fortress. An even more ambitious aircraft was initiated in the same way, identified at first as Project D, and later as the XBLR-2. Preliminary discussions to define the requirement were held with Douglas and Sikorsky in June 1935, but it was not until 8 March 1938 that construction of the selected design was authorised. The contract went to the Douglas company, covering one prototype under the designation XB-19.

This was completed in May 1941, but problems experienced in ground testing delayed the first flight until 27 June 1941, when Major Stanley M. Ulmstead and a crew of six took the giant into the air for a first uneventful and successful flight. It was then the largest aircraft built for the air force, reformed as the US Army Air Force only seven days earlier. It was to remain so for some five years, until the B-36 (q.v.) flew in 1946. Its configuration was that of a cantilever low-wing monoplane of all-metal construction, with a conventional tail unit and retractable tricycle landing gear. Quite staggering at the time were the main wheels, each 2.44 m (8 ft 0 in) in diameter. Equally outsized was the accommodation, catering for a standard crew of 16, but equipped also with eight seats and two bunks in a special compartment so that a six-man relief crew and two flight mechanics could be carried when necessary. A large galley was also provided for the preparation of hot meals during a long-duration mission. Power plant comprised four 1,491 kW (2,000 hp) Wright R-3350-5 radial engines, each driving a three-blade constant-speed propeller.

The initial flight was followed by some 30 hours of manufacturer's tests before the XB-19 was handed over to the USAAF for official trials. These were to result in a request for minor modifications and the installation of an improved braking system before the aircraft was accepted in June 1942. There had been a few other problems throughout its development programme. Most persistent was that of engine overheating, due to the aircraft being underpowered, and causing operational limitations. After being used virtually as a flying laboratory for some two years, a period which provided data that proved valuable in the design of later aircraft, the XB-19 was modified to serve as a cargo transport. At the same time, the Pratt & Whitney radial engines were replaced by four 1,939 kW (2,600 hp) Allison V-3420-11 in-line engines, and with this increased power the engine cooling problems were overcome. Used in a cargo role for some two and a half years, it was finally withdrawn from service in August 1946, and scrapped three years later.

Designed for a bombing role, the XB-19 never carried the defensive or offensive weapons that were intended for it. They included two 37 mm cannon, five 0.50 in and six 0.30 in machine-guns, and a total bombload of 16,828 kg (37,100 lb). If these weapons had been complemented by sufficiently high performance, this giant would indeed have made a useful addition to the Army Air Force's inventory.

Douglas XB-19

FARMAN
F.220-F.222

France

These were the largest bombers to serve in France between the two world wars. But, despite being totally obsolete they were used both on leaflet raids over Germany and bombing attacks once war had begun.

The prototype F.220 Bn4 was built as a thick-section, strut-braced, high-wing monoplane heavy bomber. Power was provided by four Hispano-Suiza engines mounted in tandem pairs on the lower stub wings. The fuselage was of rectangular section and, like the wings, was of all-metal construction. A first flight was achieved on 26 May 1932.

The original prototype was followed by the refined F.221 prototype, powered by four 596 kW (800 hp) Gnome-Rhône 14Kbrs radial engines. Armament included guns in manually-operated turrets in the nose and in dorsal and ventral positions. Ten production F.221s were built, each carrying a crew of five, followed by 11 F.222s. The later bombers had 14Kdrs engines, and a retractable landing gear replaced the earlier divided type. Some of the F.221s were brought up to this standard. F.221s were flown operationally from November 1936 and F.222s from April 1937.

The final bomber version of F.220 type was the F.222.2, twenty-four of which were built during 1937-38 with redesigned front fuselages and dihedral on the outer wing panels. Most were powered by 685.6 kW (920 hp) engines. Interestingly, the F.220 prototype was subsequently converted into a civil passenger/mail plane, named Le Centaure. Four F.2200 and one F.2220 airliners followed, all with Hispano-Suiza in-line engines and intended for use on Air France's South Atlantic service. The F.220 first flew from Dakar to Natal on 3 June 1935, the first of many journeys, while the F.2200s and F.2220 entered service in 1936 and 1938 respectively.

Top right: **Farman F.222** (*Musée de l'Air*)

Bottom right: **Farman** *Le Centaure*, **a civil passenger/mail conversion of the prototype F.220**

Farman F.221

FOCKE ACHGELIS
Fa 266 Hornisse and Fa 223 Drache

Germany

The work of the Spanish engineer Juan de la Cierva who, in early 1923, flew successfully his C.4 autogiro, spurred worldwide interest in the development of rotary-wing aircraft. Germany was well in the forefront of this movement, represented in particular by Professor Heinrich Focke of the Focke-Wulf company who, on 26 June 1936, accomplished a first flight of his Fw 61 design. While this was not the first practical helicopter to have flown in Europe – for the Breguet-Dorand Gyroplane Laboratoire had been demonstrated successfully exactly a year earlier – it was much superior in performance and capability to the French aircraft. Its success and promise was such that, in 1937, Heinrich Focke left Focke-Wulf to establish a new company, Focke Achgelis & Co GmbH, at Delmenhorst/Oldenburg.

In mid-1937 the Fw 61 had been used to establish a number of records: examined in retrospect some 44 years later they are still most impressive. In approximate figures they included an altitude of 2,440 m (8,000 ft), closed circuit distance of 122 km (76 miles), and an endurance of 1 hour 20 minutes 49 seconds. To Deutsche Lufthansa such capability seemed good enough to warrant the evaluation of a passenger development, and it was a contract for such an aircraft that encouraged the formation of Focke Achgelis.

Work began on the construction of three prototypes, their Fw 61 parentage readily apparent. These had the designation Fa 266 Hornisse, were to have been powered by the 626 kW (840 hp) Bramo radial engine, and would have seated six passengers. None were completed because of the outbreak of war in Europe. Instead, it was decided to adopt the helicopter for military use, with roles that included anti-submarine patrol, cargo transport, reconnaissance, rescue, and training. Thirty pre-production examples were ordered by the Reichsluftfahrtministerium, under the designation Fa 223 Drache, and the first Fa 223V-1 (D-OCEB) was flown during the autumn of 1939.

The Fa 223 had a fabric-covered steel tube fuselage, with a well-glazed flight deck in the forward section accommodating the pilot and an observer. Behind this was a cabin that could be used for cargo or up to four passengers, separated by a fireproof bulkhead from the engine compartment which, externally, was covered by metal panels. Landing gear was of tricycle configuration, and the two 12.00 m (39 ft 4 in) diameter rotors were carried on tubular steel outriggers extending from the sides of the fuselage structure. The fuselage terminated with a tail unit comprising a conventional fin and rudder, but the fin supported a strut-braced T-tailplane, the incidence of which could be adjusted. Power was provided by a 746 kW (1,000 hp) BMW Bramo 323 Q3 Fafnir radial engine.

Early testing was satisfactory, and on 28 October 1940 the first prototype was flown to a record altitude of 7,100 m (23,295 ft). Official tests also proceeded well, resulting in an order for 100 production examples, but while design and development of the Fa 223 was a success story, attempts to build production aircraft in any quantity proved to be completely frustrating. This resulted from Allied air raids which destroyed the helicopters almost as fast as they were built. By the end of the war, despite strenuous efforts in three different factories, only about a dozen had been flown and, of these, only three airworthy examples remained. It is interesting to record the farsighted plans to equip these aircraft for their operational roles, duplicating so much that has now become commonplace. They included a powered hoist for rescue operations, a load-carrying beam for the airlift of suspended external cargo, and underfuselage racks for weapons or auxiliary fuel. Immediately after the war in Europe had ended, one of the surviving Fa 223s was flown to Brockenhurst, Hampshire, so becoming the first helicopter to achieve a crossing of the English Channel.

Focke Achgelis Fa 223E Drache (Kite), the military designation of the Fa 266 Hornisse (*Pilot Press*)

FOCKE-WULF
Fw 200 Condor

Germany

Just prior to the beginning of the Second World War, the Luftwaffe Chief of Staff ordered the formation of a unit for long-range anti-shipping operations. Germany then had no aircraft suitable for such use, and neither the time, nor productive capacity, in which to produce one within the required time scale. It was decided, therefore, to investigate the possibility of adapting the Focke-Wulf Fw 200 Condor civil transport for this role.

The Condor had been designed by Professor Kurt Tank, later to become well known for design of the Fw 190. Intended for service with Deutsche Lufthansa, this was a low-wing monoplane of all-metal construction, having a retractable tailwheel type landing gear with twin wheels on the main units, and seating for 26 passengers accommodated within two cabins. Powerplant of the prototype Fw 200V-1 (D-AERE), first flown on 27 July 1937, comprised four 652 kW (875 hp) Pratt & Whitney Hornet radial engines. The next two prototypes were powered by 537 kW (720 hp) BMW 132G-1 radials, and this third machine (D-2600, *Immelmann III*) was nominated as Hitler's personal aircraft. A number of production Fw 200A/Bs were built, the majority serving with Lufthansa, but two of each went to Danish Air Lines and Syndicato Condor of Brazil.

The structure of the Condor was not stressed for military operations, so the Fw 200C that was adapted for maritime anti-shipping patrol had a strengthened fuselage structure, a powerplant comprising 619 kW (830 hp) BMW 132H-1 radials, and accommodation for a crew of five. Armament was introduced, consisting of two 7.9 mm MG 15 machine-guns in dorsal positions, and a third MG 15 and one 20 mm MG FF cannon within the ventral gondola, which was slightly offset to starboard. This also included the bomb-aimer's position and stowage for a 250 kg bomb. A maximum of six more 250 kg bombs could be carried on underwing mountings.

The Fw 200C-1 was the first version to equip Kampfgeschwader 40, the unit formed to operate the type, and these were used initially, with little success, for mine- and bomb-dropping operations against the British Isles. Subsequent versions to enter service included the C-2 with modified outboard engine nacelles and faired bomb racks; the C-3 with 895 kW (1,200 hp) Bramo 323R-2 Fafnir radials, accommodation for an additional crew member, more structural strengthening, increased bombload, and three more machine-guns; followed by four variants of the C-3 with differing weapon arrangements. Major production version was the C-4, generally similar to the C-3 but equipped with FuG Rostock search radar. Later examples could also carry FuG 200 Hohentwiel radar, which made it possible to carry out bombing attacks in darkness or through cloud. Two variants of the C-4 were equipped as 11- or 14-seat transports, sometimes used for clandestine spy-dropping operations, and one of these Fw 200C-4/U1s was the personal transport of Heinrich Himmler. Under the designation Fw 200C-6, a number of C-3/U1 and U2s were converted to carry two Henschel Hs 293 air-to-surface missiles and, in addition, a small number of aircraft were built for this missile-carrying role under the designation C-8.

Total production amounted to 276 aircraft, a surprisingly small figure when one considers the achievements of this airliner turned bomber. Known at one time as the 'Scourge of the Atlantic', Condors were responsible for the sinking of some 80 to 90 merchant ships during a six-month period of 1940-41. Measures taken by the Allies to limit the threat of these aircraft gradually began to reduce their effectiveness, but they continued to serve with the Luftwaffe for maritime operations until 1944, and in a transport role until D-Day invasion led to an end of war in Europe.

Top right: Focke-Wulf Fw 200C Condor (*Archiv Schliephake*)

Airline version of the Focke-Wulf Fw 200 Condor, operated under Lufthansa colours

GENERAL AIRCRAFT
Hamilcar

UK

In the early hours of 10 May 1940, German forces began their attack on the Low Countries, capturing first the Belgian defensive outpost of Fort Eben-Emael. This 'impregnable' post had adequate artillery to prevent an attacker from crossing the bridges of the Albert Canal: a conventional attacker, that is. The Germans chose to be unconventional, and for the first time in the history of warfare used glider-borne troops to capture key points. With the fort in German hands, additional glider-borne troops, supported by paratroops, were able to make an attack from the rear against the defenders of the canal

General Aircraft Hamilcar X, with its landing gear collapsed to unload a truck-mounted Bofors gun

bridges. Thus, the gateway to Belgium was thrown wide open.

The British government considered it to be essential that its Army and Air Force should develop a similar capability, and the training of paratroops and glider pilots was initiated in June and September 1940 respectively. The RAF's first operational troop carrying glider was the Airspeed AS.51 Horsa, and this was used operationally for the first time on 19 November 1942, when two Halifax bombers towed two Horsas, each with two pilots and 15 Royal Engineer volunteers, to attack the Norsk Hydro heavy-water plant in Norway. One Halifax and both Horsas crashed en-route, with the result that the attempt to destroy the plant was a complete failure.

Growing appreciation of the requirements of airborne operations resulted in the Air Ministry issuing Specification X.27/40, calling for a glider able to carry the heavy support equipment needed by its airborne troops. Built to this requirement was the General Aircraft G.A.L.49 Hamilcar Mk.I, the largest Allied glider to see action during

the Second World War. Designed by General Aircraft at Feltham, Middlesex, it was produced in only small numbers by the company (22), but an additional 390 were built by the Birmingham Railway Carriage & Wagon Company, leading a manufacturing group that included A.C. Cars, and the Co-operative Wholesale Society.

Designed originally to carry the Tetrarch tank, or two Universal carriers, the Hamilcar was a cantilever high-wing monoplane, mainly of wooden construction, with plywood or fabric covering. Its rectangular-section fuselage provided an unrestricted cargo hold 7.77 m (25 ft 6 in) long, with a height and width of 2.29 m (7 ft 6 in) and 2.44 m (8 ft 0 in) respectively. An enclosed flight deck, high on the fuselage and just forward of the wing leading-edge, accommodated a pilot and co-pilot in tandem. Access to it was gained – believe it or not – via a ladder inside the fuselage, through a hatch in the fuselage top surface, and via a walkway over the wing centre-section! Two types of fixed tailwheel type landing gear were available, jettisonable main units being

used when it was known or anticipated that it would be necessary to land on the underfuselage skids. The prototype was flown for the first time on 27 March 1942, and in the early hours of 6 June 1944 (D-Day) more than 70 of these big gliders took part in the overture to the Normandy landings. They were to see action subsequently at Arnhem, and during the Rhine crossings.

In the same way that the Germans had decided to power the Messerschmitt Me 321, resulting in the Me 323 (both q.v.), plans were made to power the Hamilcar so that it could operate as a conventional aircraft with rather less than half its normal payload. Powered by two 720 kW (965 hp) Bristol Mercury 31 radial engines, and intended for use in the Far East under the designation Hamilcar Mk.X, only 22 had been produced by conversion of Mk.I aircraft when the war ended.

General Aircraft Hamilcar I glider transports await their Handley Page Halifax towing aircraft (*Imperial War Museum*)

HANDLEY PAGE
V/1500

_UK_

With a skill born of subterfuge and vacillation, the British Air Board decided on 23 July 1917 that the RFC had no further need for night bombers, and postponed all orders that had been raised for experimental aircraft of this class. It was not a particularly good moment to reach such a decision, for at that time the German air force was using long-range aeroplanes to bomb the streets of London, causing an outcry from both people and Parliament. When, shortly afterward, the Air Board was confronted with the possible effects of their shortsighted decision, an immediate reversal was made, resulting in orders for 100 Handley Page night bombers (O/400s), plus six experimental heavy bombers. The latter were required for operation by night, needed to have a range of at least 805 km (500 miles), and were to comprise three large aircraft (A.3b) to carry a bombload of

Handley Page V/1500

at least 1,360 kg (3,000 lb) at a speed of 161 km/h (100 mph) and three smaller aircraft (A.2b) to carry a 227 kg (500 lb) bombload at 185 km/h (115 mph). The large aircraft, ordered from Handley Page, was to become the V/1500; the smaller version, built by Vickers as the Vimy, was to become far better known.

The Handley Page design covered the construction of what was then quite easily the largest aircraft built in Britain. A three-bay biplane, with slightly swept wings that could be folded, it was of then-standard wood and fabric construction. The long rectangular-section fuselage incorporated a nose gunner's position, with the pilot's cockpit immediately behind him; then gunners situated in dorsal and tail positions, the latter behind the large biplane tail unit. The tailskid landing gear incorporated large double mainwheel units beneath the lower wing, each side of the fuselage, and the power plant was strut-mounted between the wings, directly above these main gear units. The large size of the V/1500 had been dictated by

Handley Page V/1500 flying in the USA, where it was used once in November 1919 to carry goods for the American Railway Express Company

the need to carry ample fuel to give the required range, and also to cater for the bombload. Thus, a 4,546 litre (1,000 Imp gallon) fuel tank was built to conform with the inner shape of the upper fuselage, and the bombs were carried on racks within a bomb bay which was in the lower half of the fuselage, beneath the fuel tank.

Power plant varied, the prototype having four 280 kW (375 hp) Rolls-Royce Eagle VIII engines mounted in tandem pairs, the forward engine driving a two-blade tractor propeller, the rear engine a smaller diameter four-blade pusher propeller. The use of this smaller propeller enabled it to rotate between the upper and lower wings, without the need for a cutout in either.

The prototype flew for the first time in May 1918, resulting in a number of modifications to control surfaces and the tail unit. It was destroyed in an accident during the following month, and it was not until October that a second machine was able to continue development flying. By the time

of the Armistice, in November of that year, only three aircraft from outstanding orders for a total of 255 V/1500s had reached the RAF's No.166 Squadron, at Bircham Newton, where they were standing by to launch an attack on Berlin. Details of the number of aircraft that were completed by Handley Page and its sub-contractors appear to be far from definitive, but it seems possible that between 20 and 30 were built. Alternative engines used by sub-contractors included the 373 kW (500 hp) Galloway Atlantic and 335.5 kW (450 hp) Napier Lion IB. Armament of production aircraft comprised single or twin-yoked Lewis guns in nose, dorsal, ventral, and tail positions, and up to a maximum of 3,402 kg (7,500 lb) of bombs.

With the end of the war the V/1500 saw very limited RAF service. One was credited with the first through flight from Britain to India, between 13 December 1918 and early January 1919. A little later in 1919, this same aircraft was the only one of its type to see action when, flown by Captain Robert Halley, a number of bombs were dropped on Kabul during the trouble in Afghanistan.

95

HANDLEY PAGE
Victor

UK

Britain emerged from the Second World War with air forces that had contributed immensely to final victory. None would deny that Bomber Command's night operations had represented a significant proportion of the total effort made by the Royal Air Force. In the immediate post-war years it seemed only commonsense that procurement plans would ensure the continuity of a powerful Bomber Command, one equipped with the most advanced aeroplanes and weapons that the nation's industry could devise.

Those whose thoughts followed such lines would have gained heart-warming reassurance that all was well with Britain and the RAF when, in 1955, the first of the V-bombers entered service. This was the Vickers Valiant, to be followed by the Avro Vulcan just two years later, and finally by the Handley Page Victor, the last of

its four-turbojet V-bombers. Victors began operational service with No.10 Squadron in the spring of 1958. The V-bombers stemmed from an advanced specification, B.14/46, which had been circulated in October 1948, and this was to lead to Britain's first four-jet bomber, the Short Sperrin. However, the Sperrin was built only in prototype form, and it was the aircraft mentioned above that provided the RAF with its force of V-bombers.

German aerodynamic research had shown that swept wings and tail surfaces could help to overcome the compressibility problem engendered by flight at higher speeds. But very specific data was limited, and this is reflected in the different approach to wing design made by Vickers, Avro, and Handley Page. The latter was to adopt what became known as a crescent wing, with a progressive decrease of sweepback from root to wingtip, made in three distinct stages.

Below: Handley Page Victor B.Mk 1

Bottom: Handley Page Victor B.Mk 1 with its parachute-brake deployed

Top: Handley Page Victor B.Mk 2 in camouflage

Above: Loading a Blue Steel stand-off nuclear bomb under a Handley Page Victor B.Mk 2

Coupled with wing leading-edge flaps, and Fowler-type trailing-edge flaps, it was to result in a wing of high efficiency that could be flown supersonically in a shallow dive, but also possessing excellent low speed handling qualities.

The semi-monocoque fuselage provided accommodation for a crew of five, had a bomb bay that could contain up to 35 1,000 lb general purpose bombs or nuclear weapons, carried a swept T-tail at the rear, and was supported on the ground by a retractable tricycle landing gear incorporating twin-wheel nose units and four-wheel main bogies. Power for the initial Victor B.1 production version comprised four 48.9 kN (11,000 lb st) Armstrong Siddeley Sapphire turbojets buried in the deep wing roots. No conventional defensive armament was carried, for the Victor was intended to operate at speeds and heights that would give protection from all known defences.

Unfortunately, by the time it was ready to enter service, interceptors and missiles had been developed to an extent that height and speed alone were inadequate defence. This situation was faced by the provision of advanced electronic countermeasures and other equipment, with new or retrofitted aircraft to this standard were designated B.1A. They were to be followed by the larger and heavier B.2, with 91.6 kN (20,600 lb st) Rolls-Royce Conway 201 turbofan engines, and these could carry a Blue Steel stand-off bomb partially semi-recessed beneath the fuselage.

Despite its improvements, the B.2 was no less vulnerable to high altitude attack. Attempts were made to extend the useful life of this bomber by adopting an alternative mode of low-level attack, but by 1968 they had ceased to operate in their intended role. Variants included the strategic reconnaissance SR.2, and modified K.1/1A flight refuelling tankers. Subsequently, Mk.2s were rebuilt as K.2 tankers, these remaining in service with the RAF in 1981, but are scheduled for retirement in the mid-1980s when replaced by tanker versions of the BAC/BAe VC10.

HEINKEL
He 111Z-1

Germany

Throughout the course of the Second World War, the German aircraft industry, and related industries now embraced by the word aerospace, was responsible for a remarkable degree of innovation, much of which represented very advanced thinking. This same preparedness to adopt new ideas, or adapt existing ones for new purposes, was to lead to the appearance of some remarkable aircraft. Among this latter category of aeroplanes, the Heinkel He 111Z must come high on the list.

In 1940 there was an urgent need for an aircraft that would be able to serve as a tug for the Messerschmitt Me 321 Gigant (q.v.) which was then being developed. There had been experiments with two or three aircraft towing a single glider, but these had proved to be highly dangerous and were not regarded as practical for anything as large as the Gigant. It was Ernst Udet who first suggested the idea of uniting two bomber airframes to provide an aircraft that would be able to undertake this task, and a design study made by the Heinkel company in late 1940 showed this to be practicable. In early 1941 work began on the construction of two prototypes, with two He 111H-6 airframes each being used for the purpose. In effect, an outer wing panel, outboard of the engine, was removed from two aircraft: one port, one starboard. The two airframes were then joined together by a new centre-section, this structure incorporating an additional engine and an extra span of wing trailing-edge flap. Thus, the resulting He 111Z (Z = Zwilling = twin) had five 1,007 kW (1,350 hp) Junkers Jumo 211F-2 engines. A crew of seven was carried, the pilot in the port fuselage: he had throttles for each of the engines, flying controls, and was responsible for operating the radiator cooling flaps of the two engines on his side, and the port landing gear. The co-pilot/navigator, on the starboard side, looked after cooling of the centre and two starboard engines, and the starboard landing gear.

The two prototypes were flown successfully in the late autumn of 1941, and official evaluation, including towing trials, confirmed that the strange creation was more than capable of fulfilling the required task. This led to the construction of eight

more; three, like the prototypes, were adaptations of He 111H-6 airframes, but the remaining five He 111Z-1s were built up from He 111-H16 components, plus the new centre-section. They were equipped also to use four rockets to assist take-off with exceptionally heavy loads. The rockets comprised two of 500 kg (1,102 lb) thrust, one mounted beneath each of the original fuselage structures, plus two, each of 1,500 kg (3,307 lb) thrust beneath the new centre-section, one each side of the engine nacelle. Armament varied quite considerably, one Zwilling being known to have flown with as many as 13 machine-guns, with the crew increased by two to help operate this barrage of weapons.

The changing fortunes of war meant that although the Zwillings were easily capable of the task for which they had been intended, they had no opportunity of being deployed on a landing operation. Had this happened, their Gigants would have carried heavy support equipment and/or supplies for paratroops or troops landed by smaller gliders. They were, however, used operationally with their Gigants for supply and casualty evacuation. It is recorded that on occasions as many as 130 casualties had been carried out in a single operation: 30 on board the tug, and 100 in the Gigant.

Two projects based on the He 111Z failed to materialise: these related to an He 111Z-2 long-range bomber, and an He 111Z-3 reconnaissance version with a range of some 4,300 km (2,670 miles).

Heinkel He 111Z-1 five-engined glider tug and transport (*Pilot Press*)

HEINKEL
He 177 Greif

Germany

During the latter half of the 1930s, elements of the aircraft industry of the United Kingdom (and with a little less urgency those of the United States), were actively concerned with the development of strategic bombers. Under the promptings of Generalleutnant Walther Wever, the Luftwaffe's first Chief of Staff, a similar policy was adopted in Germany as early as 1935, leading to construction of prototypes of the Dornier Do 19 and Junkers Ju 89 four-engined long-range bombers. The most promising of these was the Ju 89, but following Wever's death in an air crash, on 3 June 1936, the programme ran out of steam and came to nothing. However, in response to a specification drawn up by the German Air Ministry, the Heinkel company submitted its He P.1041 design, and following the construction of a mock-up, in late 1937, six prototypes of this aircraft were ordered under the designation He 177.

Siegfried Günter, design leader on the project, was anxious to use only two engines, these offering better manoeuvrability and less drag than a four-engined installation, but this would have required two units each of about 1,490 kW (2,000 hp). None were available and, in fact, no engine of this output was produced in quantity by German manufacturers during the Second World War. The solution was to use four Daimler-Benz DB 601 engines, coupled in pairs, each of the resulting DB 606 units having an output of 2,013 kW (2,700 hp). This powerplant was to be responsible for many of the problems that beset the Greif. Initially, this was due to the fact that an evaporative cooling system was adopted (to eliminate conventional radiators and reduce drag), but, in parallel with Rolls-Royce experience, Daimler-Benz discovered it to be impracticable for high-powered engines with a great deal of heat to dissipate. This meant a reversion to the use of drag-inducing radiators, and generating several inter-related problems that were never resolved successfully. Thus, more drag needed increased fuel to achieve the required range: the extra fuel pushed up the gross weight, demanding a strengthened and heavier structure. The final blow, which proved to be a knock-out punch for a number of German projects, was an insistence on dive-bombing capability.

The He 177V-1 prototype was flown for the first time on 19 November 1939, a flight of short duration because the engines overheated. In configuration the Greif was a cantilever mid-wing monoplane, the wing incorporating wide-span Fowler-type trailing-edge flaps. Then-conventional all-metal construction was adopted, and the landing gear was of retractable tailwheel type, the main units each with two wheels. A crew of five could be accommodated, and basic armament comprised one 20 mm cannon and four machine-guns for defence, plus a maximum bombload of 6,000 kg (13,228 lb).

Development of the Greif brought losses from several causes, but by far the most serious problem, and one that persisted throughout the aircraft's operational career, resulted from the ease with which the engine installation could cause a disastrous fire. But, despite its shortcomings, the type was to enter service, initially in the form of the He 177A-1 with Kampfgeschwader 40. In fact, a total of more than 900 was built, the main production versions being the He 177A-1; the He 177A-3, which introduced a lengthened fuselage and armament changes; and the most extensively built (565) He 177A-5 anti-shipping/bomber version, with the Fowler flaps deleted, modified landing gear, heavier armament, and the ability to carry three mines or torpedoes.

Introduced operationally during the summer of 1942, He 177s were to be used in attacks on British and Russian targets, and against shipping in the Atlantic and Mediterranean. Had the manufacturer been given time to complete development of the Greif before it was, prematurely, pushed into operational service, there seems little doubt that the Luftwaffe would have acquired an important strategic weapon.

Heinkel He 177A Greif (*Imperial War Museum*)

HEINKEL
He 274

Germany

The development of a bomber that could operate at very high altitudes, reducing the likelihood of interception by enemy fighters, was an attractive proposition. German interest in such an aircraft led to the proposal to build a special version of the He 177 (q.v.), designated He 177A-4, which would have had a pressurised compartment for a crew of three and much reduced defensive armament. However, when interest in the proposal led to more detailed design studies, it became apparent that the resulting structure needed to be so different from that of the He 177 that it would be more realistic to create a new specific design for the changed role. As planned originally, this would have retained the He 177 fuselage structure, incorporating in it a pressurised cabin, adding a new wing of increased span. As manoeuvrability would not be quite so important at the proposed operating altitude, it was decided to eliminate the fire-prone DB 606 twin engine units. This led to retention of conventional single units of the Daimler-Benz engine, with exhaust-driven turbochargers added.

The overall concept appealed to the RLM, but because of the Heinkel company's deep involvement with the He 177 and its problems, it was decided to entrust construction and development to another manufacturer. The French company Société Anonyme des Usines Farman was to receive, in the autumn of 1941, an order for the manufacture of two prototypes and four pre-production aircraft, under the designation He 274.

These were to be developed under the supervision of Heinkel personnel, but it was not until 1943 that construction of the two prototypes began, by which time the order for pre-production aircraft had been cancelled.

At the time that work on the prototypes started, there had been a number of design changes. The fuselage, while basically the same as that of the He 177, had been lengthened, and crew accommodation increased to four; the fuselage was to be lengthened a second time during the course of construction. The tail unit comprised a wide-span tailplane/elevator, with endplate fins and rudders, the landing gear main units had been modified, and powerplant consisted of four Daimler-Benz DB 603A-2s with turbochargers. These each developed a maximum output of 1,380 kW (1,850 hp) at 2,100 m (6,890 ft), and with the turbochargers operative had an output of 1,081 kW (1,450 hp) at 11,000 m (36,090 ft). By the time that the He 274V-1 was being prepared for flight testing, in July 1944, the advance of Allied forces made it necessary for Heinkel personnel to return to Germany, first attaching demolition charges to the aircraft's engines to prevent it from being used by the enemy. These failed to cause serious damage, and the aircraft was subsequently restored to flight condition. This work was carried out by Usines Farman, by then renamed Ateliers Aéronautiques de Suresnes, with the He 274 being redesignated as AAS 01A. First flown during December 1945, the aircraft was used for a programme of flight tests, but was eventually scrapped in 1953. The second prototype was never completed.

Heinkel He 274 (*Pilot Press*)

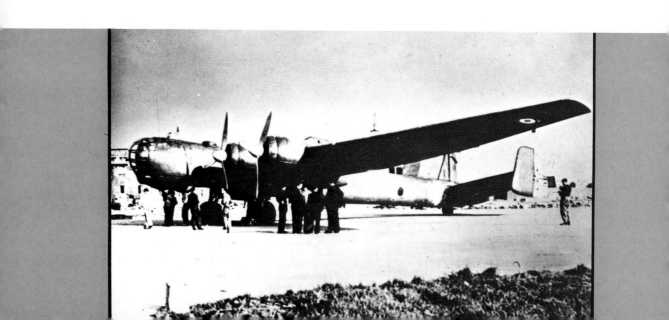

HUGHES
H-4 Hercules

USA

The H-4 Hercules remains today the largest aircraft ever flown, despite the fact that its one and only flight was made just after the end of the Second World War. Then, at the controls, was the multi-millionaire businessman, sportsman and film producer Howard Hughes.

Prior to the outbreak of the Second World War Howard Hughes had many links with aviation, including running the Hughes Aircraft Company (formed in 1936). He was also the holder of aeroplane speed and distance records, and had purchased for his own use special versions of then current airliners and civil versions of the latest USAAC fighters. Further he had built a very sleek racing aircraft with which he managed an average

speed of more than 563 km/h (350 mph) over a 3 km course on 14 September 1935.

In 1942, with America at war, he joined with Henry J. Kaiser, a prominent shipbuilder, to build three giant experimental flying-boats for the US government. Construction was to be entirely of wood, as there was concern over shortages in strategic materials, with the War and Navy Departments supplying the engines, propellers and instruments.

The government order specified that the first of these was to be completed within fifteen months for static trials, the second in 20 months and the third in 25 months for flight trials. This was by no means an easy task, especially in view of the fact that the flying-boat had been designed with a 97.536 m (320 ft) wing span and might accommodate up to 700 troops or a great amount

Hughes H-4 Hercules, the largest aeroplane ever built, here seen protected by netting (*Gordon S. Williams*)

of freight. Not surprisingly, delays and difficulties pushed back the work schedule. Preliminary tests conducted officially indicated that the complete flying-boat was likely to be very much over-weight, and this, together with the delays and the fact that the expected shortages of strategic materials had not happened, caused the project to be cancelled in early 1944 by the Aircraft and War Production Boards. However, it was suggested that one of the hulls should be completed as a mock-up to determine the feasibility of an all-metal flying-boat of similar type.

This offer did not please Howard Hughes, who decided to go it alone and personally fund one aircraft, reportedly spending more than $22 million. The completed H-4 Hercules weighed in at a staggering 181,436 kg (400,000 lb). Power was provided by eight 2,237 kW (3,000 hp) Pratt & Whitney R-4360 Wasp Major engines.

Using special trailering equipment, sections of the Hercules were transported by road from Culver City to Long Beach, California, in mid-1946, to be assembled for trials. It was launched on 1 November 1947, and on the following day,

on its third taxying test in Los Angeles harbour, the flying-boat lifted from the water for a flight of about 1.6 km (1 mile) at an altitude of 21-24 m (70-80 ft). Howard Hughes piloted the Hercules alone and without a co-pilot, and some thirty engineers, technicians and official observers were on board. In fact it was later revealed that he had not planned beforehand for the flight, but he had found the aircraft so buoyant on its previous run 'on the step' that he decided to take off. However, he later announced that he had no intention of doing any more flying with the Hercules before March or April 1948. As a result the Hercules was taken back to its hangar and later cocooned, where it remained until 1981.

Top right: Howard Hughes and crew inside the H-4 Hercules

Bottom right: The vast wing of the Hughes H-4 Hercules being transported by road

Hughes H-4 Hercules in Long Beach Harbor after its first and only flight

HUGHES
XH-17

USA

The XH-17 was a giant experimental heavy-lift helicopter, designed to prove the pressure-jet propulsion system. Built under a 1948 USAF contract, it began as a ground test model but was converted into a flight test helicopter, taking off for the first time on 23 October 1952.

Developed from the earlier Kellett XH-17 Flying Crane, the Hughes XH-17 had a gross weight 2½-times greater than any contemporary helicopter. The very large main rotor was powered by two modified General Electric GE 5500 turbojet engines, which supplied gas pressure through ducts leading up the rotor shaft and out of the tips of the blades. This system of propulsion reduced the helicopter's overall weight and complexity, as it eliminated the normal rotor transmission drive system. The helicopter's flight control system had dual hydraulics, similar to the type fitted to the H-4 Hercules flying-boat.

Capable of manoeuvring over bulky cargoes prior to take-off by virtue of its very tall and widely spaced landing gear legs, it was the forerunner of today's flying cranes. Bridge sections, portable buildings, vehicles and artillery were all within its lifting capability, and the XH-17 completed successfully its flight programme in 1953. Success of the XH-17 led to the construction of a mock-up of the expected XH-28 production version, which would have been the first helicopter capable of taking off with a gross weight twice that of its empty weight. However, because the United States was involved in the Korean War at that time, USAF allocations were used elsewhere and the XH-28 was abandoned.

Hughes XH-17 with a gigantic 39.62 m (130 ft) diameter main rotor

HUREL-DUBOIS
H.D.321

France

French aircraft designer Maurice Hurel had strong opinions regarding the efficiency of high-aspect ratio wings. Their application to provide long-range capability had been demonstrated during the war on aircraft such as the Consolidated B-24 Liberator and the B-32 Dominator (q.v.), both of which had patented high-aspect ratio wings. Soon after the end of the Second World War, Avions Hurel-Dubois was established at Meudon-Villacoublay to build a series of aircraft incorporating wings of this type. By theoretical studies, supported by wind tunnel tests, Maurice Hurel had satisfied himself that the aspect ratio of a wing could be doubled or trebled, without any increase in structural weight, provided that it was braced by suitably designed lift struts. Weight saving, combined with greater lift, promised a useful addition to an aircraft's payload without any increase in engine power.

To test the theory, an experimental monoplane designated H.D.10 was built and flown, with results that were sufficiently promising for the French government to order two larger twin-engined aircraft for further development of the concept. Designated H.D.31 and H.D.32, these were flown in January and December 1953 respectively, and subsequently a second example of the H.D.32 was built and flown. With more powerful engines installed, the H.D.32s became redesignated H.D.321-01 and H.D.321-02, serving as development prototypes for the H.D.321 cargo/passenger transport, of which the first production example flew for the first time on 22 December 1955.

Easily recognisable by its unusual braced monoplane wing, set high on the all-metal fuselage, the H.D.321 had a fixed tricycle landing gear, and a tail unit incorporating a conventional tall fin and rudder, with auxiliary endplate fins at the tips of the tailplane. Power plant consisted of two 1,137 kW (1,525 hp) Wright 982-C9-HE1 radial engines in wing-mounted nacelles, these each driving a three-blade constant-speed and fully-feathering propeller. Intended for normal operation by a crew of three, the main cabin was 12.95 m (42 ft 6 in) long, and had a maximum height and width of 2.13 m (7 ft 0 in) and 2.20 m (7 ft 2 in) respectively. It was planned for all-cargo, all-passenger, or convertible use, and could accommodate a maximum of 44 passengers.

No further examples of the H.D.321 were built, but eight generally similar aircraft incorporating only minor changes were built as photographic survey aircraft for the Institut Géographique National.

Hurel-Dubois H.D.32s

I.A.38

Argentina

On 9 December 1960 the first flight took place of the I.A.38, a large tailless monoplane cargo transport aircraft, powered by four 335.5 kW (450 hp) I.A.16E1 Gaucho radial engines mounted as pushers. It was the brainchild of Dr Reimar Horten and based on his wartime Ho VIII design for a 60-passenger flying wing airliner.

The all-duralumin two-spar semi-monocoque wing was swept back at an angle of 35° 30' and incorporated Frise-type ailerons and split flaps. Fins and balanced rudders were mounted near the wingtips. The fuselage was in and below the wing, and within the fuselage and wing could be accommodated up to 6 tons of cargo, loaded through a rear door. A troop transport version was also contemplated, as was the use of 559 kW (750 hp) I.A.19E1 Indio engines.

The I.A.38 was completed in 1959 but flight trials were delayed because of cooling problems with the engines. Once begun, it quickly became clear that the aircraft was unsuited to its task and was abandoned.

I.A.38 flying-wing transport

ILYUSHIN
Il-76

USSR

Ilyushin's Il-76 medium/long-range freight transport, which has the NATO reporting name of *Candid*, was first seen in public at the Paris Air Show in May 1971. It was designed initially to serve as a heavy transport for operation over long distances in the Siberian regions of the USSR. In addition to being suitable for operation from short unprepared airstrips, it was also required to be able to operate in severe weather conditions, and be easy to maintain.

First flown in prototype form on 25 March 1971, test and development flying continued until the basic Il-76T entered production in 1975. Its configuration is that of a cantilever monoplane, the wing mounted above the fuselage to ensure that it does not compromise cargo capacity. Because short-field operation is essential, the wing incorporates almost full-span leading-edge slats, wide-span triple-slotted trailing-edge flaps, and upper-surface spoilers forward of the flaps. Basically of circular cross-section, the fuselage is of all-metal fail-safe construction, carrying a tail unit with all-swept surfaces that incorporate a variable-incidence T-tail. The retractable tricycle landing gear is designed to keep wheel loadings as low as possible, the nose unit having two pairs of wheels side by side, and the main units each with two four-wheel units in tandem. When retracted, the main units are housed in two large ventral fairings beneath the fuselage, again ensuring that these structures do not impede cargo loading or compromise capacity. Power is provided by four 117.7 kN (26,455 lb st) Soloviev D-30KP turbofan engines, each mounted in underwing pods.

The Il-76 is operated by a crew of seven, with the pilot and co-pilot side by side on the flight deck. The navigator is accommodated beneath them, in a glazed nose station, reportedly to enable him to give visual assistance in the selection of landing sites. The entire crew and cargo accommodation is pressurised. Cargo loading is via clamshell doors in the upswept rear fuselage and a hydraulically-actuated ramp, and advanced mechanical handling equipment is provided for containerised and other freight. Quick-change modules, of which three can be carried, are each able to accommodate 30 passengers, stretchers and medical attendants, or cargo.

In addition to operating with Aeroflot, Il-76Ts are reportedly in service with Iraqi Airways, Libyan Arab Airlines, and Syrianair. They are used as transports by the Soviet Air Force, and are expected to enter service also in AWACS (Airborne Warning And Control System) and flight refuelling tanker roles. The capability of the Il-76 in a transport role was demonstrated at an early date, initially on 4 July 1975 when, piloted by Yakov I. Vernikov, it raised 70,121 kg (154,590 lb) to record the greatest payload carried to a height of 2,000 m. In all, 24 records for speed and altitude with payload were established. Also in 1975, a team of Soviet parachutists carried in an Il-76 raised the world record for a high altitude jump to 15,386 m (50,479 ft).

Ilyushin Il-76 (*Tass*)

Ilyushin Il-76T (Tass)

ILYUSHIN
Il-86

USSR

Although the Soviet Union has been active in producing a range of transports suitable for operation by both Aeroflot and the Soviet Air Force, the Il-86 (NATO reporting name *Camber*) is its first wide-body transport in the mould of the US 747/DC-10/TriStar, and the European Airbus. As early as 1971 it was known that Ilyushin had an aircraft of this class in the project design stage, and in the following year a model was displayed in Moscow showing a layout similar to that of the Il-62, with four rear-mounted engines and a T-tail. Up until that time, Ilyushin's proposal had been in competition with submissions from the

Ilyushin Il-86 photographed at the Paris Air Show (*Brian M. Service*)

Antonov and Tupolev design bureaux, but it was the Il-86 that was chosen for development to production standard. In this process, the design team realised that the proposed rear-engined layout would impose severe weight penalties and so, instead, chose to use the underwing pod installation.

In overall configuration, the Il-86 is very similar to the European Airbus, differing by having a four- rather than two-engine installation and by being slightly larger in size. Both have an alternative nine-abreast high-density seating layout to accommodate a maximum of 345 and 350 (Il-86) passengers. Even powerplant is relative, for the combined output of the two high-powered turbofans of the Airbus is only some seven per

Ilyushin Il-86

cent below that of the four Soloviev turbofans on the Il-86.

Almost inevitably, because it is designed for a similar role to the wide-body jets in service outside the Soviet Union, the wing has the same degree of sweepback, and incorporates basically the same high lift devices. The circular-section fuselage is designed for pressurisation, and terminates in a large conventional tail unit with all-swept surfaces. The retractable landing gear is of the multiple type, with a nose unit having twin wheels, and three main units each with a four-wheel bogie. An interesting feature of the cabin layout is provided by passenger doors which incorporate airstairs, and hinge downward from the port side of the lower deck. They enable passengers to embark or disembark without the need for any ground equipment. Having entered the aircraft, passengers can stow coats and hand baggage in lower deck cloakrooms, before climbing one of three internal staircases to gain access to the main deck.

The first flight of a prototype was made on 22 December 1976, and almost exactly four years later, on 26 December 1980, the type entered service with Aeroflot on its Moscow-Tashkent route. Services between Moscow and Mineralnye Vody were being operated in early 1981, and it was reported that Aeroflot intends to introduce this airliner on some 27 other major domestic routes. Future plans for this excellent aircraft are reported to include the development of a long-range version with more powerful engines, having an estimated range of 6,000 km (3,725 miles).

JUNKERS
G 38
and
MITSUBISHI
Ki-20

Germany/Japan

The first G 38 airliner took to the air for its maiden flight on 6 November 1929. It was a truly remarkable aeroplane, with huge cantilever monoplane wings of very thick section, covered with corrugated metal. The rectangular-section fuselage was a semi-monocoque structure, also constructed of metal, as was the biplane tail unit. Power was provided initially by two 298 kW (400 hp) Junkers L-8 and two 559 kW (750 hp) Junkers L-88 engines (ending with four 559 kW; 750 hp Junkers Jumo 204s), installed in the leading-edge of the wings and so arranged that they could be attended to in flight. But perhaps the most interesting feature of the aeroplane was its passenger accommodation, which eventually provided for 26 passengers in the main fuselage cabins, three in each of two cabins in the wing roots and two in the extreme fuselage nose.

Only two G 38s were built. The first was named *Deutschland* and the second *Generalfeldmarschall von Hindenburg*. Both were operated by Deutsche Lufthansa; the first was lost in an accident in 1936 and the second was destroyed in 1940 during a bombing raid by the RAF.

So successful was the G 38 that Japan decided to produce the K-51 heavy bomber derivative in secrecy, having previously obtained a licence for it from Junkers. Intended to be capable of reaching the Philippines from bases outside Japan, a total of six was built by Mitsubishi as Ki-20s, completed between 1931 and 1934. These were tested by the Army as the Type 92 heavy bomber but proved unsuccessful and were therefore not employed on any of Japan's military campaigns of the latter 1930s.

Top right: Junkers G 38 with the original mixed engines driving two- and four-blade propellers

Middle: Mitsubishi Ki-20

Bottom right: Mitsubishi Ki-20

Junkers G 38 *Generalfeldmarschall von Hindenburg*

JUNKERS
Ju 322 Mammut

Germany

Although the outcome of the Battle of Britain had resulted in the shelving of German plans to invade the UK, it was emphasised by Adolf Hitler's headquarters staff that this was regarded as a postponement rather than a cancellation. That this was so was confirmed to some extent very shortly afterwards, when the development of truly giant gliders was initiated. These were intended to airlift heavy equipment for the first wave of the assault and, alternatively, would accommodate more than 100 fully-equipped troops.

Specifications of the RLM's requirements were drawn up and issued to both Junkers and Messerschmitt in late 1940, these covering two designs. One was of steel-tube basic structure, the other of wood: unfortunately for Junkers, which had no experience of wood construction, it was the recipient of the all-wood specification. This was to present very real difficulties for the company, for its lack of experience in wood constructional techniques, coupled with problems in obtaining timber of sufficiently high quality, resulted in the finalisation of a design with a payload some 20 per cent below that demanded by the specification. It was to get worse, rather than better, for during the trial loading of a PzKw IV tank, this slipped from the loading ramp and tipped forward, seriously damaging the cargo floor. When a strengthened floor had been introduced, to prevent a recurrence, the design payload had been reduced by 44 per cent.

In configuration the Mammut was basically a flying wing, for the comparatively short fuselage served only to carry the tail unit. The wing incorporated a very deep centre-section, this

serving as the cargo hold, and loading was accomplished from the front of the aircraft through detachable leading-edges that gave access to almost the full width of the hold. The pilot was accommodated in an enclosed cockpit just aft of the leading-edge, offset to port, and defensive machine-guns were mounted in three positions, two just outboard of the removable leading-edge access panels, and one on the upper surface of the fuselage, adjacent to the wing trailing-edge. It was planned that the glider would land on four sprung skids, with wheels beneath the forward gun positions to prevent the leading-edge from digging-in during a rough landing. The realisation of a suitable launch trolley that could cope with the weight of the glider and its cargo had presented some problems. As finalised, it was a heavy steel tube structure with eight pairs of wheels. This was attached to the skids for take off, and could be jettisoned once the glider had gained a suitable height.

Despite the problems faced by Junkers, the Ju 322 was ready for testing in April 1941, towed off on its first flight by a Junkers Ju 90. The launch trolley was wrecked when it hit the ground after being jettisoned, and the Mammut was so unstable under tow that it seemed both tug and glider would be destroyed. In desperation the glider pilot dropped the tow rope, and immediately his charge became perfectly stable, enabling him to make a successful landing some distance away. From there, the glider was retrieved by a pair of tanks some two weeks later, these towing it back to the airfield.

Despite efforts made by Junkers to improve flight performance, the RLM decided to abandon the project in favour of the alternative Messerschmitt design. Both prototypes, and 98 partially-built airframes, were cut up and used as fuel for wood-burning vehicles.

Junkers Ju 322 Mammut glider

JUNKERS
Ju 390

Germany

Following the Japanese attack on Pearl Harbor, and America's entry into the Second World War, Germany's Reichluftfahrtministerium began to pay attention to the creation of a capability to launch bombing attacks from Europe against America's eastern coastline. The plan was, initially, to put bomber aircraft over New York, but as a growing range capability was developed there would be no shortage of attractive targets. The specification of an aircraft to fulfil this role was issued to the Focke-Wulf, Junkers, and Messerschmitt companies, and faced with this requirement the Junkers design office proposed an enlarged version of the Ju 290 strategic bomber, itself derived from the Ju 90.

In configuration the Ju 390 was a cantilever low-wing monoplane of all-metal construction, but extensive use was made of Ju 290 components. By comparison with its predecessor it had an increased-span wing centre-section, a lengthened fuselage, a generally similar tail unit incorporating considerable tailplane dihedral that resulted in inward-canted endplate fins and rudders, and a tailwheel type landing gear with four main units, each with twin wheels. It was intended that for normal operation the two inboard main units would be used, all four being required only when the aircraft was being loaded to its maximum gross weight. Power was provided by six 1,268 kW (1,700 hp) BMW 801D radial engines, mounted in wing leading-edge nacelles, each driving a three-blade propeller.

Three prototypes had been ordered for transport (V-1), maritime reconnaissance (V-2), and heavy bomber (V-3) roles. The Ju 390V-1 was built at Dessau, and was flown for the first time during August 1943. The Ju 390V-2, built at Bernburg, differed by having a longer fuselage, was equipped with FuG 200 Hohentwiel radar, and carried an armament of four MG 151 20 mm cannon and three MG 131 machine-guns. The third prototype was never completed, and plans to put it into production as the Ju 390A long-range heavy-bomber failed to materialise.

The Ju 390 differed conspicuously from many unrealised projects of the combatant nations by demonstrating, most effectively, that it had the capability intended for it. During January 1944 the Ju 390V-2, which could carry sufficient fuel for an endurance of approximately 32 hours, was flown from Mont de Marsan, near Bordeaux, to a position some 19 km (12 miles) from the US coastline, just north of New York, before returning to its base without incident.

Aware of the development of this aircraft, Japan's Army Air Force was very interested in the V-3 long-range bomber version, and a manufac-

turing licence was negotiated. However, the end of the war in Europe came before these plans were implemented. Had the Ju 390A been built, it would have been a formidable bomber, powered by BMW 801E engines, each of 1,469 kW (1,070 hp), and carrying a defensive armament of six MG 151 20 mm cannon, and four MG 131 machine-guns. Underwing racks were to be provided for weapons that could include bombs or missiles, and it was estimated that with a weapons load of 1,930 kg (4,255 lb), this version of Junkers' giant bomber would have had a range of some 9,200 km (5,720 miles).

Junkers Ju 390V-1

JUNKERS
Ju 88 Mistel Composites

Germany

The concept of the Mistel (Mistletoe) composites represents another example, similar to that of the Heinkel He 111Z-1 (q.v.), of German readiness to adapt existing aircraft for a totally different role if it was expedient to do so. In this case, however, the requirement was very different from that of the He 111Z, for development of the Mistel composites (called sometimes Vater und Sohn = father and son) resulted from the need to find a means of launching an aircraft loaded with explosives against a vital target. The idea was not new, and in any case it evolved from attempts that were being made to develop ways in which two aircraft, towed or mechanically interconnected, could complement each other. The British pre-war Short-Mayo composite (q.v.) was typical of this line of thought.

In early 1943 the RLM ordered from Junkers a prototype of this idea, which would combine an unmanned Junkers Ju 88 bomber, representing a bomb or missile, with an attached and manned Bf 109 that would guide the heavy weapon to its target. Chosen for the initial tryout of this concept was a Ju 88A-4 and a Bf 109F-4.

Comparatively little work was needed on the fighter airframe, but it was necessary to devise a strutted structure for installation on the bomber to which the Bf 109 would be attached. The prototype combination was completed by July 1943 and, flown for the first time towards the end of the month, was found to be completely practical.

In its developed configuration, the fighter was supported above the Mistel at its wing centre-section by two tripod structures, which were attached to the Ju 88's main wing spars. A single strut was provided at the fighter's tail, and could be disconnected by the pilot of the upper com-

Junkers Ju 88 Mistel composite stands abandoned on the runway of Bernburg airfield, Germany, together with another Ju 88 minus the Focke-Wulf Fw 190 upper component, following its destruction by aircraft of the US 8th Army Air Force (*US Air Force*)

Close up of a Mistel 2, with a temporary nose fitted to the Ju 88 for delivery, prior to having a hollow-charge warhead fitted (*Imperial War Museum*)

ponent. This strut was spring-loaded, and as it was compressed it completed a circuit, releasing catches that secured the fighter to the main attachment points of the tripods which could be explosively or mechanically disconnected. For take-off, and for flight prior to release of the Mistel, the combination could be flown on the power of the Ju 88's two engines, the engine of the fighter being stationary and the propeller feathered. It was more usual, however, to fly on the power of all three engines, the fighter drawing its fuel supply from the tanks of the Mistel. When the objective was reached, the pilot would aim the Ju 88 at its target, flying as close to it as prudent, and then disconnecting and returning to base. This was the weak point of the concept, for while the Ju 88 would continue in stable flight, under control of an onboard autopilot, it was not guided from the moment of release. Wire- and television-guidance schemes were investigated to eliminate this shortcoming, but their realisation was frustrated by the end of the war.

Production conversions needed little work on the upper component, and a number of designations resulted from the use of different combinations of fighter/bomber. Thus the Mistel 1 (and S 1 training version) united the Ju 88A-4 and Bf 109F, the Mistel 2 (and S 2) the Ju 88G-1 and Focke-Wulf Fw 190A-8, and Mistel 3A (and S 3A) the Ju 88A-6 and Fw 190A-6. The designations Mistel 3B and 3C applied respectively to longer-range versions in which Ju 88G-10 or Ju 88H-4s were directed by an Fw 190A-8 with overwing auxiliary fuel tanks.

Work carried out on the Ju 88s was, of course, far more comprehensive, for apart from the structural changes to unite the two aircraft, there was a complete refit of equipment, the addition of extra fuel tankage, and the provision of means to attach the 3,500 kg (7,716 lb) hollow-charge warhead which was the essential feature. This had an impact fuse, primed automatically after separation, and testing had shown its steel core to be capable of penetrating some 18.5 m (60 ft 8 in) of concrete. Despite such potential, deployment of the Mistel proved to be most frustrating, due primarily to the fact that the weapon was unguided after separation, but enjoyed some degree of success against bridges and other targets on the Eastern Front.

121

KAMOV
Ka-22 Vintokryl

USSR

Receiving the NATO reporting name *Hoop*, the Ka-22 was one of the surprises to observers at the 1961 Soviet Aviation Day Display. It was a very large convertiplane, which the commentator described as the most powerful vertical take-off machine in the world.

Power was provided by two 4,192 kW (5,622 ehp) Soloviev TV-2 turboshaft engines in wingtip pods, each with a tailpipe that could be tilted downward for additional lift in vertical flight. These drove four-blade rotors during take-off, landing, hovering and low-speed flight, and forward-facing four-blade propellers during cruising flight (when the rotors autorotated). The entire trailing-edge of the wings comprised ailerons and flaps. The fuselage was approximately the same size as that of the Antonov An-12 fixed-wing transport, capable of accommodating 80-100 passengers, vehicles or freight. Loading of freight was facilitated by a ramp incorporated into the upswept tail. Interestingly, this convertiplane can be regarded as the forerunner of the Mil V-12 and Mil Mi-26 helicopters in terms of role, as the later helicopters were also designed to give VTOL mobility matched to fixed-wing transport capacity.

On 7 October 1961, the Ka-22 set up a class E.2 convertiplane speed record of 356.3 km/h (221.4 mph) over a 15/25 km course, a record which stands today. On 24 November of the same year, it lifted a payload of 15,000 kg (33,069 lb) to a record altitude of 2,588 m (8,491 ft), qualifying also for records with a payload of 1,000, 2,000, 5,000 and 10,000 kg. On the same day, it lifted 16,485 kg (36,343 lb) to an altitude of 2,000 m (6,562 ft). It remained an experimental type.

Right: **Kamov Ka-22 Vintokryl**

Kamov Ka-22 Vintokryl (*Novosti*)

KAWANISHI
H6K

Japan

In 1933 the Imperial Japanese Navy advised the Kawanishi Aircraft Company, which had been founded only five years earlier, of a requirement for a large flying-boat suitable for such duties as maritime patrol, reconnaissance, and transport. Initial design studies proved unacceptable, and resulted in the Navy issuing a revised specification that was even more demanding. This called for an ambitious cruising speed of 222 km/h (138 mph), allied with a range of 4,633 km (2,879 miles). However unimpressive this may now appear to be, it represented a capability which, if achieved, would be superior to that of the Sikorsky S-42, a US flying-boat used by Pan American Airways in the pioneering of its trans-oceanic routes.

The resulting Kawanishi Type S (as designated originally by the company), was designed by a team headed by Yoshio Hashiguchi and Shizuo Kikahura. They were among Kawanishi personnel that had been entertained earlier in Britain by Short Brothers, where they had gained a valuable insight into the design and construction of waterborne aircraft. When the prototype, which by then had the company designation H6K1, made its first flight on 14 July 1936, it was seen to be a large parasol-wing 'boat with four 626 kW (840 hp) Nakajima Hikari 2 radial engines in nacelles at the leading-edges of the wings. A stabilising float was strutted and braced beneath each wing, and the hull was of two-step design, providing accommodation for a crew of nine. Early flight testing of the prototype resulted in modifications to the hull design to improve on-water performance, and when service trials showed that this had been satisfactorily achieved,

Kawanishi H6K4-L transport

three more prototypes were ordered. These had Hikari 2 engines originally, but the first prototype and the third and fourth of these new aircraft received 746 kW (1,000 hp) Mitsubishi Kinsei 43 radials before entering service under the designation Navy Type 97 Flying-Boat Model 1. Production eventually totalled 215 aircraft (including prototypes), and comprising 10 generally similar H6K2 Model 11s; two H6K3 personnel transports; 127 H6K4 Model 22s, the major production version, later examples with Kinsei 46 engines; and 36 H6K5 Model 23s with either Kinsei 51 or 53 engines of 969 kW (1,300 hp).

There was also a separate line of development for pure transport use. Two of the H6K2s served as prototypes, equipped to provide accommodation for 18 passengers, with a galley, and mail and cargo compartments. As a result, 16 H6K2-L and 20 H6K4-Ls were built and, in addition, two

more H6K4-Ls were produced by the modification of two H6K4s.

When war in the Pacific began, in late 1941, a total of 66 H6K4s was in first-line service with the Japanese Navy, these being allocated subsequently the Allied codename *Mavis*: similarly, the transport H6K4-Ls became codenamed *Tillie*. In addition to deployment in their primary operational role for long-range maritime reconnaissance, H6K4s were used also to bomb land targets, carrying up to 1,000 kg (2,204 lb) of bombs, but for these latter operations their lack of armour protection and self-sealing fuel tanks, and limited defensive armament, made them extremely vulnerable to Allied fighters. When operating in maritime reconnaissance or transport roles, where there was less likelihood of encountering enemy fighters, they proved to be most effective. Many of the Navy's transports, and the civil versions used by Greater Japan Air Lines, remained in service until the end of the war.

Kawanishi H6K5 (*US Air Force*)

KAWANISHI
H8K

Japan

Early evaluation of the H6K by the Imperial Japanese Navy gave an appreciation of that flying-boat's limitations, and resulted in the issue of a far more demanding specification. Calling for a maximum speed of 444 km/h (276 mph) and maximum range of 8,339 km (5,182 miles), representing performance superior to contemporary flying-boats of British and US origin, it led to the design, development and production of the Kawanishi H8K. By the war's end the type had gained an excellent record, and early post-war evaluation in the US left little doubt that this aircraft had hydrodynamic and performance characteristics superior to any other wartime flying-boat produced by the combatant nations.

Faced with the need to create a flying-boat that was destined, in major production form, to exceed all of the Navy's requirements except in terms of range, Kawanishi decided that it would not prove adequate to come up with an aircraft that was merely a development of the H6K. Instead, the team headed by Shizuo Kikahura evolved a completely new design, incorporating a two-step hull of very narrow cross-section, and a cantilever monoplane wing mounted in a high-set configuration. Although it had been the original intention to use a retractable stabilising float beneath each wing, the need to restrict overall weight resulted in a strutted and braced installation, similar to that of the H6K. However, the retractable float installation was later incorporated in two H8K3 prototypes of 1944, these two aircraft being developed in an attempt to increase maximum speed.

Kawanishi H8K2 photographed in July 1944, seconds before being shot down by US aircraft (*US Air Force*)

Kawanishi H8K2 (*Smithsonian Institution*)

As with its predecessor, the H8K had four engines in nacelles at the wing leading-edges. Mitsubishi MK4A Kasei 11 or MK4B Kasei 12 radials of 1,141 kW (1,530 hp) powered the prototype and production H8K1s, but 1,380 kW (1,850 hp) MK4Q Kasei 22s were used for H8K2 and H8K2-L production aircraft and the H8K3 prototypes. With the need for long range, a large capacity fuel system had been designed. While this included a number of unprotected small capacity wing tanks, the bulk of fuel storage was in partially self-sealing hull tanks, and these were provided with a carbon dioxide fire-extinguishing system.

Armament of early production aircraft consisted of a 20 mm cannon in dorsal and tail turrets, plus five 7.7 mm machine-guns in beam blisters, ventral, cockpit, and bow positions. The major production H8K2 had this increased to a total of five 20 mm cannon and four 7.7 mm machine-guns, making it the most heavily armed flying-boat to see service during the Second World War. In addition to these defensive weapons, all production aircraft (other than those intended for a transport role) could carry an external weapon load comprising two 800 kg torpedoes, eight 250 kg bombs, or sixteen 60 kg bombs or depth charges.

The first flight of the prototype H8K1 was made during January 1941, and leading to major hull modifications to correct very unsatisfactory on-water performance. Although this work gave much improvement, the hydrodynamic stability of the H8K was never as good as that of its predecessor, but both flight characteristics and performance were much superior. Production of this ten-crew 'boat, under the official designation Navy Type 2 Flying-Boat Model 11 (H8K1), was authorised in late 1941. Allocated the Allied codename *Emily*, the type was first used operationally at the beginning of 1942.

Production of H8Ks, totalling 167, included 36 H8K2-L personnel transports. These were able to accommodate 29 passengers on two decks, made possible by the deep hull, or a total of up to 64 troops could be carried. Built in only small numbers by comparison with the patrol flying-boats used by the Allies, a fact which resulted from Kawanishi being directed to concentrate on the production of fighter aircraft, the H8K is remembered in Japanese aviation history as its best and largest flying-boat.

LATÉCOÈRE
521, 522 and 523

France

On 17 January 1935 the Laté 521 flying-boat flew for the first time. Powered by six 641 kW (860 hp) Hispano-Suiza 12Ybrs twelve-cylinder V engines, four driving tractor propellers and two driving pusher propellers and with the inner pairs in tandem, it was a very large strut-braced sesquiplane. Seating was provided for 70 passengers on trans-Mediterranean services and 30 on transatlantic, with maximum main hull accommodation for twenty passengers in the first saloon, followed by six de luxe sleeping compartments, a saloon for 26 passengers, a kitchen and second toilet. A compartment for a further 18 passengers was situated in the superstructure, aft of the flight deck.

Following successful tests with the Laté 521 named _Lieut de Vaisseau Paris_, orders for three improved civil and three military versions were placed in 1935. However, the Laté 521 sunk at its moorings at Miami in early 1936 while making a circuit of the Atlantic. Luckily it was saved, thereafter being returned to France for reconstruction. When it reappeared in the following year, it was powered by 485 kW (650 hp) Hispano-Suiza 12Nbr engines. As well as being used on

Latécoère 521

several long-distance flights, this flying-boat established a number of load-over-distance and load-to-height records.

Although three other similar flying-boats had been ordered for commercial use, and certainly at least two were under construction for Air France at one stage, the only other commercial version was the Laté 522. Powered by 671 kW (900 hp) Hispano-Suiza 12Y37 engines, the outbreak of the Second World War prevented its use on regular transatlantic services. Named _Ville de Saint-Piérre_, it differed from the Laté 521 in several ways other than powerplant, the most obvious being its redesigned and less angular bow, with a new forward compartment that reached the extreme nose of the hull. After a period of impressed service with the French Navy, alongside the Laté 521, the Laté 522 returned to passenger services in March 1940. However, both of these flying-boats were destroyed by the retreating Germans in August 1944.

Of the military examples ordered in 1935, the French Navy received all three Laté 523s between January and October 1938. Each was armed with five 7.5 mm Darne machine-guns and could carry 1,200 kg (2,645 lb) of bombs. Maximum endurance was an impressive 33 hours. These were used for Atlantic patrols with Escadrilles E6 and E12 until one was sunk in September 1939, and a second was scuttled in June 1940 to prevent its capture. The third was grounded in August 1942, having flown with Escadrille 4E out of Dakar since mid-1941.

LATÉCOÈRE 631

France

The Latécoère 631 design dated from 1938, when the French Air Ministry ordered a prototype flying-boat for transatlantic services. It had to be capable of carrying 40 passengers over 6,000 km (3,728 miles) against a 60 km/h (37 mph) headwind. Construction was interrupted during 1939-40 by the outbreak of war in Europe, but the prototype was completed while France was under German occupation and flew for the first time on 4 November 1942. Later, the aircraft was confiscated by the German forces of occupation and taken to Friedrichshafen, on Lake Constance, where it was eventually sunk during an Allied bombing raid.

In 1942 two more Laté 631s were ordered, but a total of nine was eventually laid down after the war at the St Nazaire works of SNCA de Sud-Ouest. The first six were for delivery to Air France. Of these, the first three were each fitted with six 1,193 kW (1,600 hp) Wright GR-2600-A5B engines, while subsequent aircraft had higher-rated R-2600-C14BB engines. The first of these went into service with Air France on the transatlantic service between Biscarosse and Martinique from 26 July 1947, but following the loss of one of the flying-boats on a delivery flight and another over the Atlantic in 1948, Air France withdrew its Laté 631s from service.

Efforts were made to find a use for the remaining flying-boats. No 8 in the series was modified as a freighter, capable of carrying 20 tons of freight over a range of 3,000 km (1,864 miles) or 22 tons over 2,500 km (1,550 miles). It received its C of A from the Bureau Veritas in August 1949, and in the same month it flew from Biscarosse to Abidjan, Ivory Coast, with an intermediate stop at Port Etienne, under the livery of Société d'Exploitation du Matériel Aéronautique Française (SEMAF). This company had been formed in early 1949 to operate Laté 631s over routes to Africa, Indo-China, South America, etc. However, in 1950 No 8 met with an accident, after which plans to use further Laté 631s were abandoned. Several of the unused flying-boats were destroyed in their hangars during freak weather.

Latécoère 631

Above Latécoère 631

The French Sud-Est SE 200 six-engined flying-boat was ordered in 1936 from Lioré et Olivier for transatlantic commercial services. Four were built. The two completed during the Second World War were seized by the German forces but destroyed during RAF bombing raids. The other two were completed after the war as 80 passenger (40 by night) flying-boats, rivalling the Latécoère 631s for size

LAWSON
L-4

USA

The Lawson Airplane Company had a brief career, which ended around 1922 with the part destruction of its L-4. This was a giant 24-passenger airliner, intended to go into service with the Lawson Airline Company on a night run between New York and Chicago, for which the airline held a US Post Office contract.

Developed from the twin-engined L-2, the L-4 was conventional in all but size, with fabric-covered wooden wings and an all-wooden fusel-age. The biplane-type tail unit had what was described as a 'trimming plane' in front of it, to counteract the considerable centre of gravity shifts that would be incurred with such a large passenger cabin. Power was provided by three 313 kW (420 hp) Liberty 12 engines, two mounted between the wings and one in the fuselage nose, all driving two-blade propellers. Referred to in 1922 as the most complete airliner ever built, the L-4 had sleeping berths, a shower bath, toilet and many other refinements for passenger comfort. Unfortunately, the field selected in Milwaukee for its first trial flight was totally unsuited to such an aircraft, and when the pilot tried to attain a take-off it was partially wrecked. Although every hope was expressed of getting the L-4 repaired, the accident brought about the end of the aircraft and company.

Lawson L-4

LINKE-HOFMANN
R.I. and R.II

Germany

Linke-Hofmann was a large railway car manufacturing and general engineering company. During the First World War it played a part in supporting German aviation, and two original aircraft of giant size are of particular interest. Both were designed as a result of the inspection department of the Flying Service trying to create competition between Zeppelin, AEG, Siemens-Schuckert and other companies. The later of the two types was the L.H.W. R.II, which looked like a conventional single-engined biplane until it is realised that it

had a wing span of 42.1 m (138 ft 4¼ in), an all-up weight of 12,000 kg (26,455 lb), could attain 130 km/h (81 mph), and that its single 7 m (22 ft 8 in) diameter propeller was driven by four 194 kW (260 hp) Mercedes D.IVa engines grouped in the fuselage. Another interesting feature of the R.II was the landing gear, in which the wheels were constructed of steel with wooden tyres, supported on a multi-spiral spring shock-absorbing device. Although two R.IIs were constructed, it is believed that only one was flown postwar. After a flight, and to avoid landing in heavy snow on the aerodrome, the R.II landed in an adjacent marsh and rolled through two ditches before coming to rest. The wheels sunk 30 cm (12 in)

Linke-Hoffmann R.I

into the marsh without causing the aircraft to overturn. Finally, the R.II was fitted out experimentally as a twelve-passenger airliner.

Far more curious in design than the R.II was the R.I, designed again as an experimental heavy bomber and also failing to get beyond prototype stage. This aircraft made use of an enormous fuselage, the size of which was largely the result of tests conducted in the wind tunnel at the Göttingen laboratory, which showed that a body entirely filling the interplane gap gave better overall lift to drag ratio on the whole machine than did one which only partly filled the gap. The lack of continuity between the results of tests with the model and those with the full-size aircraft is interesting, especially in view of the fact that subsequent tests with models of similar design, made postwar at the NPL, again showed that the design was practicable. As for the actual R.I, two prototypes were built. The first flew in early 1917 but broke up in the air in May of the same year when the biplane wings collapsed. The second R.I. introduced certain refinements and indeed was said to have excellent manoeuvring qualities, although the machine was slow in answering to its ailerons and difficult to land as the pilot sat so high. This R.I also crashed, marking the end of development. Like the R.II, the R.I. used four Mercedes engines in the fuselage, but this time driving two propellers mounted between the wings.

Linke-Hoffmann R.II

LOCKHEED
C-141 StarLifter

USA

Lockheed's C-141 StarLifter is not only a big aeroplane, it had the distinction of being the first pure-jet strategic transport to be designed for the USAF. Considering it necessary to modernise the aircraft equipping the Military Air Transport Service, now Military Airlift Command (MAC), especially in terms of providing enhanced capability, the USAF issued to industry its requirements in this respect. Proposals were received from Boeing, Convair, Douglas, and Lockheed, but it was the latter company's design that was selected for development in March 1961, then designated as Support System SS476-L.

The initial contract covered the production of

Lockheed C-141A StarLifter alongside the prototype C-141B

five aircraft, by then designated C-141A and to which the company added the name StarLifter. The first of these was flown on 17 December 1963, when its relationship to the C-130 Hercules was very clearly apparent. However, it differed not only in being larger, but by having a swept wing to gain the full benefit of its high-performance turbofan engines. These comprised four 93.4 kN (21,000 lb st) Pratt & Whitney TF33-P-7s, pylon-mounted in individual pods below and forward of the wing leading-edge. The other conspicuous change replaced the conventional tail unit of the Hercules with a tall T-tail.

Following official testing, which showed that the C-141A effectively met requirements, subsequent contracts were to bring total production to 285. The first of these aircraft entered service

YC-141B StarLifter

at Tinker AFB on 19 October 1964, and in April 1965 MAC introduced the type into operational service. Within a few months of that date, StarLifters were operating a regular service to and from Viet-Nam, taking out essential supplies and troops, and returning wounded servicemen to the USA. These operations were to show the desirability of providing the type with an in-flight refuelling capability: they had also made it clear that limitations on loads were being made by cubic capacity rather than weight. To put it another way, in the majority of cases the StarLifter was able to carry more weight than space would allow. It seemed sensible to investigate the means of providing increased capacity.

Studies carried out by Lockheed showed that a fuselage 'stretch' of 7.11 m (23 ft 4 in) could be

made without the need to introduce any modification to the landing gear, powerplant, or wing structure. Work on a prototype conversion was initiated, and the resulting YC-141B made its first flight on 24 March 1977. Simultaneously with the work on the fuselage, flight refuelling capability was incorporated. The first production conversion, designated C-141B, entered service with MAC in December 1979, and it was planned to complete conversion of all MAC's in-service StarLifters (271) by mid-1982. It is interesting to consider the effects of this fuselage stretch, which makes it possible for the C-141B to carry three more standard pallets than its predecessor. Calculations based on the increased capacity show that the USAF will have the equivalent of adding 82 aircraft to its StarLifter fleet when the conversions have been completed, and this discounts the increased utilisation provided by having a flight refuelling capability.

LOCKHEED
C-5A Galaxy

USA

The growing importance of ample and suitable transport capability had been well impressed upon the USAF in the years that followed the Second World War. Signposts, such as the Berlin Airlift and Korean War, pointed directly at these aircraft, which made possible the short-term movement of large volumes of essential cargo, and/or the rapid deployment and subsequent support of troops far from their home base. In 1963 the USAF's Military Air Transport Service, now Military Airlift Command (MAC), began to consider the development of a transport much larger than the Lockheed C-141A StarLifter and Douglas C-124 Globemaster II (both q.v.) that were then in service.

Inter-service discussions led to the CX-HLS requirement, calling for the capability to carry a 56,699 kg (125,000 lb) payload over a range of 12,875 km (8,000 miles), and these details were circulated in May 1964. From the submissions, Boeing, Douglas, and Lockheed were awarded contracts to develop their designs, leading to selection of Lockheed as prime contractor. Construction of the prototype, by then designated C-5A and named Galaxy, began in August 1966. Just less than two years later, on 30 June 1968, the prototype was flown for the first time. Like the majority of transports, it is a cantilever high-wing monoplane, this configuration chosen to ensure that the wing structure does not compromise cargo capacity. A tall T-tail is mounted at the rear of a fuselage that needs to be seen to be believed. A 'visor' type upward-hinging nose and ramp allows vehicles to drive in or out of the forward end; an under-fuselage rear loading door and ramp provides the same facility at the tail. Between these loading ramps is an unrestricted hold 36.91 m (121 ft 1 in) in length and 5.79 m (19 ft) wide. It can accommodate practically any item of the US Army's current equipment and, for example, has carried two M48 tanks, weighing

Prototype Lockheed C-5 Galaxy, the world's largest aeroplane

some 89,811 kg (198,000 lb), over transoceanic ranges.

Power for the Galaxy is provided by four 182.3 kN (41,000 lb st) General Electric TF39-GE-1 turbofans in individual underwing pods, but the landing gear represents a vital and complicated feature of this aircraft's design. The nose unit has four wheels, and the four main units each have a six-wheel bogie. All the wheel units have a normal extended position for take-off and landing, but also have a ground capability of being 'kneeled' to simplify loading and unloading of cargo. In addition, they can be turned up to 20° port or starboard to allow for crosswind operation, and all tyres have in-flight deflation capability.

The flight deck, high in the nose and on the upper floor, accommodates the normal crew of five. To the rear of the flight deck is a rest area for up to 15 relief crew members, and in the rear area of the upper floor, aft of the wing carry-through structure, there is accommodation for 75 troops.

When used as a personnel transport, an additional 270 fully-equipped troops can be carried on the lower deck.

When introduced into operational service in 1970, the C-5A was then dimensionally the largest in-use aircraft in the world. Despite this factor, its introduction into service presented few problems, and C-5As were soon being used regularly and reliably to carry supplies to Viet-Nam. Since then they have continued to be a major asset to MAC, able, with the use of flight refuelling, to operate to any point in the world, even with a maximum payload. The cloud on the Galaxy horizon was provided by wing structure fatigue that threatened to bring early retirement. As a result, Lockheed was awarded a USAF contract in early 1978, covering the manufacture of two new sets of wings for the C-5A. Of virtually new design, and intended to reduce stress and increase service life to 30,000 hours, they have since been tested successfully. A contract for the construction of production wing sets was awarded in January 1981, and it is planned to replace the wings of the 77 in-service Galaxies during the period 1982-1987.

Lockheed C-5A Galaxy

Unloading a giant Lockheed C-5A Galaxy (*Brian Mackenzie Service*)

LOCKHEED
L-1649A Starliner

USA

There are few who would argue with a widely expressed opinion that, for a short period of time before the world's civil airlines became dominated by turbine-powered aircraft, the L-1649A Starliner was the queen of the air. It, and the Douglas DC-7C Seven Seas, were top of the league; but for sheer beauty of line the Starliner got the extra votes that took it to the head of the list.

It had a long history, the construction of a prototype Constellation to meet a TWA order beginning in 1940. But when this flew for the first time on 9 January 1943, America had been at war for just over two years, and, as Constellations came off the production line, they were adopted for service within the USAAF. It was not until 5 February 1946 that TWA was able to inaugurate a New York-Paris service, flown by the Constellation *Star of Paris* (NC86511), piloted by Captain Harold F. Blackburn and carrying 35 passengers.

From that time forward there was steady improvement of the type, with the first major change coming in 1950 when the original prototype Constellation was converted to serve as the prototype L-1049 Super Constellation. This differed from the standard aircraft primarily by having the fuselage lengthened by 5.59 m (18 ft 4 in), representing the largest single 'stretch' given to any piston-engined aircraft. At the same time, there was a general strengthening of the entire airframe to cater for the higher operating weights, a considerable increase in fuel capacity, and the installation of more powerful engines. When first flown it was found to have excellent flight characteristics, but the powerplant which

Lockheed Starliner in TWA livery

had been installed, comprising four 2,013 kW (2,700 hp) Wright R-3350-CB1 radials, was still inadequate. Because of this shortcoming only 24 were built. But the next civil version, the L-1049C, had a turbo compound version of this engine, developing a maximum of 2,242 kW (3,250 hp) for take-off.

The Starliner was evolved to meet a TWA request for a slightly longer-range version of the Super Constellation, to counter the challenge of the long-range Douglas DC-7C. An increased span wing was designed for the prototype conversion, this containing the additional fuel needed to provide the extra range: at the same time, the fuselage was given a final 'stretch' of 0.79 m (2 ft 7 in). The introduction of this wing moved the inboard engines further away from the cabin and this, coupled with slower-turning propellers and a higher standard of soundproofing, gave the

Starliner a much-improved cabin environment. Other improvements included redesigned landing gear and the introduction of new powered controls.

In its new form, the L-1649A Starliner flew for the first time on 11 October 1956. A crew of five was carried normally for transcontinental flights, but up to 11 were used on long-range transoceanic routes. Standard first-class accommodation was provided for 58 passengers, but up to 75 could be carried in a high density tourist class arrangement. The type entered service with TWA in June 1957, but was to enjoy a comparatively short period of supremacy before being challenged by the first of the new turbojet-powered airliners in late 1958.

There are still many people alive who look back on the days of the flying-boats with nostalgia. There is another generation that has a very similar feeling about the Super Constellation/Starliner family. Both seem to represent a more gracious age of travel that may never be repeated.

Lockheed Starliner

LOCKHEED
R60-1 Constitution

USA

Interest shown by Pan American in the development of a new Lockheed long-range transport was frustrated by American involvement in the Second World War, following the Japanese attack on Pearl Harbor. Lockheed's design had introduced a figure-of-eight or 'double-bubble' fuselage, the two partial rings of the figure eight

One of the first post-war double-deck transports was the Lockheed Constitution

meeting at a tension diaphragm which served as the upper deck. In a civil version this would have been used for the accommodation of passengers, the area below the passenger cabin providing ample baggage/cargo space.

US Navy interest in this design, identified by Lockheed as their Model 89, was to result in a contract for two prototypes. Allocated the designation XR60-1, the first of these made its maiden flight on 9 November 1946. A low-wing cantilever monoplane of all-metal construction, the wings incorporated Fowler-type trailing-edge flaps, and had powered controls. A conventional tail unit was mounted on the somewhat unconventional fuselage, and the retractable tricycle landing gear also had an unusual feature. The twin wheel nose unit was conventional, but each

142

main unit comprised two oleo-pneumatic struts, each carrying twin wheels. Power was provided by four 2,610 kW (3,500 hp) Pratt & Whitney R-4360-22W radial engines, each with two turbochargers and driving a four-blade constant-speed and reversible-pitch propeller with a diameter of 5.84 m (19 ft 2 in). For naval use these aircraft, which acquired the name Constitution, were operated by a crew of 12 that, in addition to a captain, pilot, and co-pilot, included a navigator, radio operator, two flight engineers, two orderlies, and three relief crew members. Service personnel were carried on both decks, the upper catering for 92, and the lower for 76 on troop seats: the two decks were linked fore and aft by spiral staircases. Passenger access was gained normally through a door on the port side of the fuselage, aft of the wings, but if no ground equipment was available, personnel could be embarked or disembarked via a stairway in the nosewheel well.

There was a considerable degree of sophistication in installed equipment and systems. The landing wheels were spun up before landing; the engines, which were accessible in flight via wing tunnels, had fire detection and fire extinguishing systems; and the galley included refrigerators and deep-freeze storage units. Operated as R60-1 Constitutions, both served as transports with Navy Squadron VR-44 until 1955.

Lockheed Constitution towers above a 1936 Lockheed Model 12

MacCREADY
Solar Challenger

USA

Dr Paul MacCready and his design team first hit the news headlines when, on 23 August 1977, his Gossamer Condor man-powered aircraft became first in the world to fly a figure-of-eight course around two pylons that were 0.8 km (0.5 miles) apart). This same team's Gossamer Albatross made the first man-powered crossing of the English Channel. Flown on 12 June 1979, from Folkestone, England, to the beach of Cap Gris Nez, France, this involved a straight-line distance of 37 km (23 miles). The aircraft was piloted and powered by Bryan Allen, who had also provided the power source and guidance for the earlier Gossamer Condor. The cross-Channel flight, flown at an average speed of about 21 km/h (13 mph), involved 2 hours 49 minutes of non-stop pedalling for Bryan Allen, and represented a magnificent achievement.

But apart from the physical effort that had propelled this quite large aircraft (28.60 m; 93 ft 10 in wing span) across a formidable natural barrier, the creation of such a large heavier-than-air vehicle, robust enough for the task and yet weighing only 31.75 kg (70 lb) without its pilot, represented a giant aviation achievement. Perhaps the realisation of these two great goals would have been enough for most men. Not for Paul MacCready. He was still anxious to create a solar-powered aircraft that would be good enough to establish a significant flight. He did not imagine for a moment that a day would dawn when the sky would be filled with rush-hour traffic of solar-powered aircraft, carrying proud owners to and from the office. His primary aim was to demonstrate to the world the growing capability of solar cells, and to spur further development that might make them more effective, and far cheaper to buy.

To this end he began the design of such a vehicle, using for his initial experiments a man-powered aircraft named Gossamer Penguin, a three-quarter scale version of the Albatross. It was provided with an electric-motor to drive the propeller, but used an electric battery as a source of power for some 50 experimental flights. This was followed by the installation of a solar panel that could be tilted to gain maximum power from each cell when the sun was low on the horizon, which was the normal condition for all early flights, carried out in the calm of the morning, soon after sunrise. The first successful solar-powered flight was recorded with Gossamer Penguin on 18 May 1980, when a short climbing flight was made on solar power alone. It was to be followed by a flight of about 3 km (2 miles) on 7 August 1980, which was good enough to encourage development of the purpose-built solar-powered aircraft.

Named Solar Challenger, this soon began to take shape. Sponsorship was from the Du Pont Company, which was able to give help with the advanced lightweight materials used in its construction. Of cantilever high-wing monoplane configuration, it has an unusual aerofoil section, cambered below and flat above, as is the tailplane, these making ideal mounting surfaces for the 16,128 solar cells that provide the power source. They are capable of providing a maximum output of 2.25 kW (3.0 hp) at sea level, and this current is fed directly to an electric motor without any intermediate storage battery. The Astro electric motor is rated at 2.05 kW (2.75 hp), and this drives a two-blade variable-pitch tractor propeller constructed of Styrofoam and carbonfibre. A deep but narrow fuselage/gondola mounted beneath the wing provides accommodation for the pilot, and carries beneath it a small nylon nosewheel and a bicycle monowheel. The tail unit, mounted on a tailboom, includes a fixed-incidence tailplane with an elevator, and a fin and rudder.

A number of battery-powered test flights preceded the first solar-powered flight, made on 20 November 1980, and only two weeks later a flight of 1 hour 32 minutes was recorded. The 'giant' achievement of this aircraft was a first solar-powered crossing of the English Channel, on 7 July 1981. Piloted by Steve Ptacek, the airborne distance of 188 miles (302 km) was completed in a non-stop flight of 5 hours 23 minutes, representing an average speed of almost 56 km/h (35 mph).

MacCready Solar Challenger (*Martyn Cowley*)

MARTIN
Models 130 and 156

USA

Glenn L. Martin, one of America's pioneer pilots and aircraft builders, had established his own company at an early date. He subsequently merged with the Wright Aeronautical Company, founded by the Wright brothers, to form the Wright-Martin Aircraft Corporation at Los Angeles, California. A number of aircraft of his design were produced under the Wright-Martin name before, in 1917, he withdrew from the association and reformed his own Glenn L. Martin Company at Cleveland, Ohio. In 1929, he occupied a new factory in Baltimore, Maryland, on a site which had been chosen carefully to combine room for expansion with adjacent facilities for the launch and operation of flying-boats. A growing demand for Martin aircraft made further expansion imperative, and among additions made in 1937-38, the company erected a 137.16 m by 91.44 m (450 ft by 300 ft) assembly building for the new flying-boats which had become an important part of their activities.

The Martin 130 Clipper, although built in only small numbers, proved to be an outstanding aircraft, and in the late 1930s the company initiated the design of a new flying-boat which, it was hoped, would provide even better performance over intercontinental ranges. Designated as the Model 156, it incorporated ideas resulting from experience. The 130 and 156 were both of high-wing configuration, with the wing centre-section braced to the hull on each side, but the wide span outer panels were free from struts or bracing. Special trailing-edge flaps, of Martin design, were incorporated in the wing, and were used to provide reduced take-off runs and slower landing speeds. Each two-step hull was of an advanced type, developed after the completion of extensive testing of models in a hydrodynamic tank. Underwing stabilising floats and/or conventional sponsons were replaced by short stub aerofoil surfaces on each side of the fuselage, known to the company as seawings. In addition to providing stability on the water, they were intended to assist at take-off and, once the aircraft was airborne, they made some contribution to the total lift of the wings. The 156's strut-braced tail unit incorporated twin fins and rudders, and power was provided by four 746 kW (1,000 hp) Wright GR-1820-G2 Cyclone radial engines, mounted in wing leading-edge nacelles.

The Model 156 was intended for operation by a crew of five, housed in a flight deck high in the bow of the hull, with the pilot and co-pilot side by side, and the navigator, radio operator and flight engineer behind them. Accommodation within the cabin was for a maximum of 46 passengers, but provisions were incorporated for the cabin to be converted to 'sleeper' accommodation if a reduced number of passengers was carried.

Although test flown successfully, the outbreak of war brought an end to development of the 156, for the company had to concentrate instead on the design and large-scale production of military aircraft which became well known under the names Baltimore, Marauder, Mariner, and Maryland.

The 48 seat Martin Model 130, with 618 kW (830 hp) Pratt & Whitney R-1830 Twin Wasp engines

MARTIN
Model 275 SeaMaster

USA

However exciting was the sight and thunder of a huge turbojet-powered patrol flying-boat making its take-off run, viewed in retrospect it was a true anachronism. Perhaps the US Navy had exactly the same feelings about the Martin Model 275 SeaMaster, procured initially as the XP6M-1. For although prototypes and pre-production aircraft were built, the production contract was cancelled after the completion of three. In a modern navy, assuming that it numbers aircraft carriers among its fleet of vessels, there can be very few occasions when the use of a specialised water-borne aircraft is justified. Nevertheless, no pains were spared to ensure that this somewhat revolutionary aircraft

Martin XP6M SeaMaster

would not fail for want of the most advanced equipment. It was given, in addition, provisions for the installation of extra equipment able to provide multi-role capability, rather than restricting its operations merely to those of a maritime patrol aircraft.

Two XP6M prototypes were ordered following approval of Martin's design. Each was configured as a cantilever high-wing monoplane, but here, immediately, was a notable difference from earlier designs. Instead of wings high above the water surface, those of the SeaMaster had pronounced anhedral which, combined with acute sweepback, brought the wingtips so close to the water surface that the stabilising floats were made an integral part of the wingtip structure. The single-step hull was of all-metal construction, and introduced Martin-developed 'hydroflaps' beneath each side of the hull. Operated differentially they served as water rudders, but could be deployed collectively for use as a water brake. All-swept tail surfaces included a conventional fin and

rudder, a tailplane and elevators with pronounced dihedral being mounted on top of the fin. Powerplant of the two prototypes comprised four 57.8 kN (13,000 lb st) Allison J71-A-4 turbojets, these being nacelle-mounted in pairs above the wings, adjacent to the hull. These nacelles incorporated hinged, full-length panels, intended to make engine changes possible when the SeaMaster was afloat.

The flying-boat was designed for operation by a crew of four: pilot, co-pilot, navigator/minelayer, and a radio operator. All four were accommodated on a pressurised flight deck, provided with a pressure lock that made it possible for a crew member to leave the flight deck at any time to gain access to an unpressurised area of the hull. Aft of the flight deck was a mine bay, the lower hull structure of this section incorporating a rotary water-tight 'mine-door' on which mines, stores, or a reconnaissance camera pod could be installed. It was intended that to speed turnaround under operational conditions, this door would be removed at the flying-boat's base, and replaced by one already loaded with the required weapons. Standard installations included an APU, air-conditioning, anti-icing, advanced nav/com avionics, and radar.

The XP6M-1 prototypes, first flown on 14 July 1955 and 18 May 1956, were both lost subsequently in flying accidents attributed to shortcomings in design of the tail unit.

Six YP6M-1 pre-production aircraft had been ordered, these powered by J71-A-6 turbojets, but modifications to the tail unit delayed considerably their entry into service. Production aircraft, of which 24 were ordered in August 1956, carried the designation P6M-2. These were powered by Pratt & Whitney J75 turbojets, each with an output of some 76.5 kN (17,200 lb st), but production was cancelled after only three had been completed.

Below: **Martin XP6M SeaMaster taxiing at Martin's Baltimore seadrome**

Bottom: **Martin XP6M SeaMaster showing the engine and rear armament installations**

MARTIN
XPB2M-1 Mars

USA

The largest flying-boat to serve with the US Navy, a prototype of the Martin Model 170 Mars had been ordered on 23 August 1938 under the designation XPB2M-1 (experimental patrol bomber). By the time it had made its maiden flight, on 3 July 1942, the US was involved in the Second World War, and evaluation was to bring a decision not to proceed with production of the Mars in the patrol bomber role for which it had been designed.

In configuration, the prototype was a cantilever high-wing monoplane of all metal construction, with stabilising floats mounted beneath each wing. The massive single-step hull was upswept at the rear, mounting a dihedral tailplane with endplate fins and rudders. Powerplant consisted of four 1,491 kW (2,000 hp) Wright R-3350-18 Duplex Cyclone radial engines, these being mounted in nacelles at the wing leading-edge. A

The Martin XPB2M-1 experimental patrol bomber, from which the JRM Mars cargo transport flying-boat was developed

flight deck, providing an excellent field of view, was positioned on the bow of the hull, and in its planned role the Mars would have been operated by a crew of 11.

Considered unsuitable for operation as a patrol bomber, the Mars was modified in December 1943 for service as a cargo transport. Redesignated XPB2M-1R, it was flown in this form in late December, with a telling demonstration of its capability being made in early 1944. This involved the delivery of a 9,299 kg (20,500 lb) cargo load from the US to Hawaii, the round trip of some 7,564 km (4,700 miles) completed in 27 hours 26 minutes. This, and similar operations, was to result in an order, in January 1945, for 20 similar cargo transports under the designation JRM-1. These were to have reinforced floors, larger hatches to improve loading access, and the provision of loading equipment. The twin-tail was replaced by a conventional unit with a single tail fin and rudder, and powerplant consisted of more powerful 1,715 kW (2,300 hp) Wright R-3350-8 radials.

Production ended after only six had been built, five as JRM-1s, plus a single JRM-2 operating at the higher gross weight of 74,843 kg (165,000 lb). At a later date the JRM-1s were converted to operate at this higher gross weight, being redesignated as JRM-3s.

Martin JRM-1 Mars

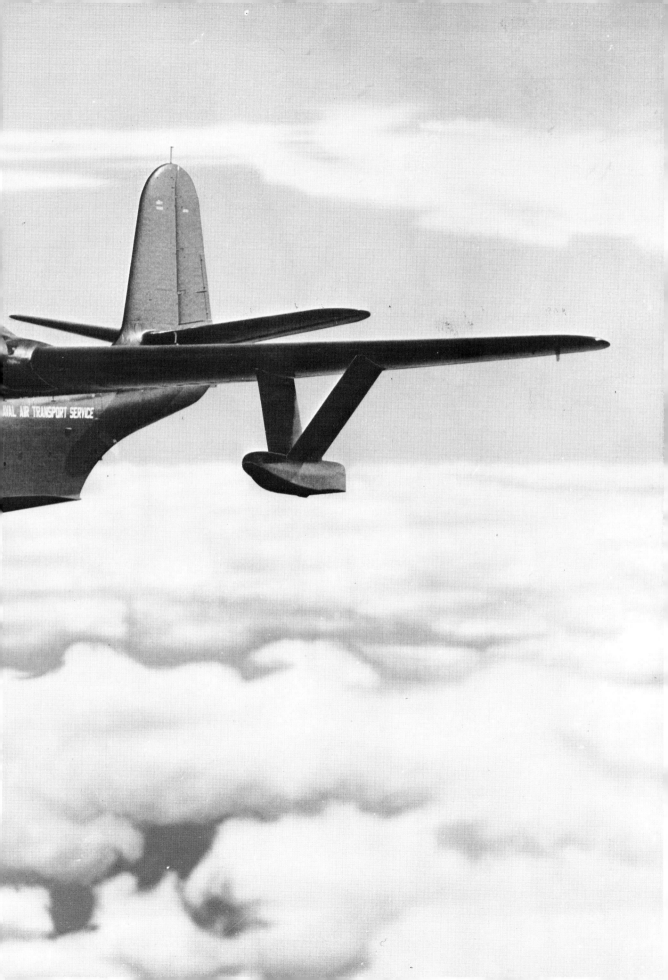

MAXIM
1894 Biplane

UK

Well-known for the machine-gun bearing his name, which he invented while resident in Britain, former American citizen Sir Hiram Maxim also has a place in British aviation history for the design and construction of a giant aeroplane. Strictly speaking, this should not be so called: more accurately it was a test rig, with which Hiram Maxim sought to explore the possibility of achieving a controlled degree of lift.

Prior to building the 'biplane', he had experimented with the design of wings and propellers, testing the efficiency of different models on a whirling-arm rig. Having formulated some ideas for the shape of his aircraft, he began the development of the powerplant that it would need. This was to take the form of a lightweight compound steam engine that was amazingly advanced for its day and which, fed with steam at a pressure of 22.5 kg/cm (320 lb/sq in), had an output of 134.2 kW (180 hp). Two of these engines were required to power the giant test rig, which Maxim created at Baldwyn's Park, Bexley, in Kent, each driving a pusher propeller that was 5.44 m (17 ft 10 in) in diameter.

Basically of biplane configuration, the outer wing panels had very pronounced dihedral. Fore and aft of the wings were two monoplane surfaces that served as elevators. The entire contraption was united by a maze of struts and wire bracing, mounted upon a frame or undercarriage. This was supported on four steel wheels, enabling the 'biplane' to run along a railway track

Maxim's 1894 biplane

One of the huge steam-driven propellers from Maxim's biplane

extending for 549 m (1,800 ft). Running along each side of the track was a wooden guard rail, these being above small outrigger wheels mounted on each side of the undercarriage so that if, on test, the 'biplane' should become airborne, it would be restrained after lifting about 0.61 m (2 ft) from the rails.

The total lifting surface of this rig was about 371.6 m² (4,000 sq ft), and its weight, complete with the undercarriage and a three- or four-man crew, was 3,629 kg (8,000 lb), giving a wing loading of approximately 9.77 kg/m² (2 lb/sq ft). The last of three test runs, made on 31 July 1894, was to demonstrate that Maxim's design had lifting capability. With the boiler at full pressure, he opened the throttles for the two engines, and the 'biplane' began to move down the track. After travelling for about 183 m (600 ft), the giant

became airborne, all four outrigger wheels engaging the guard rails. Unfortunately, an axle of one of the outrigger wheels sheared under the load, and the undercarriage immediately fouled the wooden rail. Maxim closed the steam valve, and that was that.

Sir Hiram Maxim had achieved what he set out to do, proving that even this 3,629 kg (8,000 lb) test rig could be lifted into the air. Without the guard rail it might have risen higher, but proper flight would have been impossible as there was no way of controlling the 'biplane' in flight. Perhaps the strangest factor of all was that after achieving this initial success, Maxim took no further interest in the project, and failed to develop it beyond this test rig stage. Perhaps the cost had been too great, for he is reported to have said that the project had cost £30,000 of his own money – a very big sum indeed in 1894. Ironically, some fifteen years later he built a far more conventional biplane which ought to have flown, but didn't!

McDONNELL DOUGLAS
DC-8

USA

A giant of its time, the prototype Douglas DC-8, America's second turbojet-powered airliner, towers above earlier Douglas piston-engined airliners

In the late 1930s, immediately prior to the outbreak of the Second World War, the Douglas DC-3 held the lion's share of the US commercial transport market. The same pattern was followed post-war, and for the first decade Douglas and Lockheed had a virtual monopoly. Lockheed Constellations and the Douglas DC-7 (338 built) represented the pinnacle of achievement of piston-engined civil transports. Thus, in the early 1950s the company was actively persuing the development of a successor to the DC-7. It was to take the form of a turbojet-powered aircraft, seen to be similar in general configuration to the new Boeing Model 707 when it was flown for the first time on 30 May 1958. Its configuration was that of a cantilever low-wing monoplane, the swept wing incorporating leading-edge slots, two-section ailerons, double-slotted trailing-edge flaps,

and wing upper-surface spoilers. The circular-section fuselage was constructed for pressurisation, and carried a conventional tail unit with all-swept surfaces. The tricycle landing gear incorporated twin nosewheels, with a four-wheel bogie on each main unit, and power for the prototype was provided by four 57.8 kN (13,000 lb st) Pratt & Whitney JT3C-6 turbojets. Designated DC-8, the first to fly was the initial domestic model, identified as the Srs 10, and this gained Certification on 31 August 1959. Thus, by the time that it entered service with Delta and United Air Lines, on 18 September 1959, Boeing's 707 had gained a sales lead that the DC-8 was never able to pull back. DC-8 versions which entered service subsequently were the Srs 20, with more powerful turbojets, intended for domestic operations from hot and high airfields. More important was the Srs 30 which followed,

The larger McDonnell Douglas DC-8-63 in Iberia livery

the first true intercontinental version, with more powerful engines, increased fuel capacity, and operating at a higher gross weight. The generally similar Srs 40 differed by having Rolls-Royce Conway turbofans, and introduction of Pratt & Whitney JT3D turbofans produced the Srs 50. These initial versions provided accommodation for between 117 and 189 passengers, according to layout. The Srs 50 was also available in convertible passenger/cargo or all-cargo configuration, this being known as the Jet Trader.

High sales figures for the Boeing 707 did not result only from the fact that it was earlier on the market, but also because from the outset, the Boeing company adopted a more flexible approach to varying customer requirements. In an attempt to compete more effectively, McDonnell Douglas introduced in 1966 the DC-8 Sixty Series, these providing various combinations of fuselage

'stretch' and payload/range performance. Comprising Srs 61, 62, and 63 versions, all three were also available in convertible configuration, identified by the suffix CF, and the Srs 62 and 63 were available for all-freight (AF) operations. When production ended in 1972, a total of 556 of all versions had been built.

More recently, the company has initiated a programme to re-engine DC-8 Srs 61, 62, and 63 aircraft. With General Electric/SNECMA CFM56 turbofan engines installed, with which the company stated these aircraft would have a noise reduction of about 70 per cent, they are redesignated Srs 71, 72, and 73 respectively. The initial Srs 61 conversion was flown in its Srs 71 form for the first time on 15 August 1981. In addition to this programme, the company has also begun a modification line to convert passenger transports for service as specialised freighters. This involves the removal of passenger installations, and their substitution by a seven-track cargo floor, a cargo loading system, and with cabin windows replaced by metal plugs.

MESSERSCHMITT
Me 264

Germany

Development of Messerschmitt's four-engined Me 264 was originated to satisfy the RLM's requirement for a long-range bomber which, like the Junkers Ju 390 (q.v.), was required to make attacks upon US targets from European bases. Like the de Havilland Mosquito, that was developed in Britain, Messerschmitt's design was based upon a bomber that would avoid interception by relying upon speed and altitude. However, by the time the first of three prototypes had made its maiden flight, in December 1942, the United States had become involved in the war, so the RLM had drawn up new specifications for this long-range bomber that demanded defensive armament, plus a heavier bombload than that envisaged by the Messerschmitt design team. Calculations soon showed that this increased payload could only be achieved by the installation of six engines. Therefore, although proposals were put forward to the RLM for an Me 264B version with a powerplant comprising six BMW radials, the Junkers 390 (q.v.) proved to be more attractive, since its construction was based on the utilisation of many Junkers 290 components.

However, the decision not to adopt the Messerschmitt long-range bomber proposal did not mark the end of the Me 264, for the company was ordered to develop the two unfinished prototypes for evaluation in an extremely long-range reconnaissance role. Theoretically, the Me 264 would have proved ideal for this purpose because, designed as it was for high-speed high-altitude operations, it had extremely clean lines that had been adopted to keep drag to an absolute minimum. In configuration it was a cantilever high-wing monoplane, the aircraft having swept and tapered wing leading-edges, a circular-section fuselage with an extensively-glazed crew compartment, and a variable-incidence dihedral tailplane with endplate fins and rudders. Retractable tricycle landing gear, with single wheels on each unit, and four 1,268 kW (1,700 hp) BMW 801D radial engines in wing-mounted nacelles, completed the external appearance of the second (Me 264V-2) prototype. Installation of essential armament and equipment proved to be protracted, and it was not until late 1943 that the aircraft was almost ready for initial pre-flight ground testing.

Above: Close-up of the Messerschmitt Me 264

Right: Messerschmit Me 264 (*Archiv Schliephake*)

At that point the factory was damaged in an Allied bombing attack, and the prototype destroyed. Work on the V-3 airframe continued, but this was never completed due to an acute shortage of strategic materials, which meant that priority for supplies of structural metals and a wide range of equipment went instead to in-production interceptors and V-weapons that, it was hoped, would turn the tide of war before the Allied advance had reached a point that was irreversible.

MESSERSCHMITT
Me 321/323 Gigant

Germany

The entry for the Junkers Ju 322 Mammut (q.v.), outlines the reasons for German development of giant gliders. To meet the same requirement that produced the unsuccessful Ju 322, Messerschmitt made a proposal on rather more conventional lines. When, at the beginning of November 1940, the two companies were ordered to begin urgent manufacture, Messerschmitt was instructed to use a steel-tube basic structure, and consequently had far fewer production difficulties than Junkers. Whereas this latter company's programme was littered with problems from beginning to end, Messerschmitt's proceeded comparatively smoothly.

Designated originally as the Me 263, this glider was redesignated in production form as the Me 321A, and named Gigant, before the Me 321V-1 prototype was first flown on 25 February 1941, just less than four months from receipt of the initial order. In configuration the Gigant was a braced high-wing monoplane of mixed construction, with both wing and fuselage basic structure of welded steel tube. Wing contours were maintained by wooden ribs, the leading-edge plywood covered, the remainder fabric covered; those of the fuselage were formed by secondary wood fairings, with the whole of it then fabric covered. The entire braced wooden-structure tail unit was hinged to the fuselage to allow for 7.5° of variable incidence. Landing gear, like that of the Ju 322, consisted of four sprung skids, but Messerschmitt had contrived a more practical four-wheel dolly, which was jettisoned as soon as the glider had gained a suitable height.

Accommodation for the pilot, who was the only crew member, was in an enclosed cabin, high on the fuselage and forward of the wing leading-edge. Beneath him was the cavernous hold of the Gigant, with loading access gained via clamshell doors in the nose, and doors on each side of the fuselage. Unusual features were a cargo floor stressed to almost double the empty weight of the glider, and provision for an intermediate deck that made it possible for the Gigant to carry a maximum of 200 troops. Production of 100 Me 321A-1s was followed by about 100 Me 321B-1s. These differed by having a wider flight deck to accommodate a pilot and co-pilot,

and as many as four additional crew could be carried to act as loadmaster, radio operator, and gunners for the standard armament of two MG 15 machine-guns.

Towing was carried out usually by a Junkers Ju 290A, or Heinkel He 111Z, but if neither of these were available there was the rather dicey alternative of a trio of Bf 110s. To help a heavily laden Gigant into the air provision was made for the attachment of booster rockets, and to slow it on landing a ribbon parachute could be streamed from the rear fuselage. Never deployed in their intended cross-Channel invasion role, the Me 321s saw only limited use in logistic support missions on the Eastern Front. These operations emphasised the fact that without a self take-off capability these aircraft were of little use. This was to spur development of the powered Me 323 Gigant, with Me 323V-1 and V-2 prototypes having four and six engines respectively. It was considered that four engines would be enough to keep the Gigant airborne after take-off with towed assistance. This was true, but didn't eliminate the towing problems. In most instances the six-engined V-2 could operate as a conventional powered transport, and it was this version that was to be built to the tune of more than 200 examples.

In addition to the installation of engines and related systems, the Me 323s had structural strengthening, plus non-retractable ten-wheeled bogie landing gear, and because it was envisaged that they would frequently operate unescorted, they carried comparatively heavy defensive armament. Production versions, comprising Me 323D and Me 323E variants, were powered by six 850 kW (1,140 hp) Gnome-Rhône 14N 48/49 radial engines. Entering service in late 1942, they were used initially on trans-Mediterranean routes, providing logistic support to the Afrika Korps, but were to suffer heavy losses. They were deployed subsequently in a logistic/evacuation role on the Eastern Front.

Messerschmitt Me 323 Gigant

MIL
Mi-26

USSR

The Mi-26, known to NATO as *Halo*, is a new very large heavy lift helicopter, with much greater capacity than the Mi-6 and Mi-10. Suited to military and civil applications, its cargo hold is 15 m (49 ft 2½ in) long, 3.20 m (10 ft 6 in) wide and 3.15 m (10 ft 4 in) high, in fact similar in size to that of a Lockheed C-130 Hercules fixed-wing transport. Inside the hold, about 40 tip-up seats are provided along the walls for troops or work crews accompanying freight loads. The maximum internal or external payload is reported to be 20,000 kg (44,090 lb); a rear-loading ramp, clamshell upper rear doors and two 2,500 kg (5,511 lb)-capacity electric winches on overhead rails facilitate loading.

An Mi-26 was exhibited at the 1981 Paris Air Show, and was said to be one of several prototypes or pre-production aircraft. It is thought that development of the helicopter has been completed and that production is imminent or has already started. Power is provided by 8,500 kW (11,400 shp) Lotarev D-136 free-turbine turboshaft engines, driving a single eight-blade main rotor.

Mil Mi-26, the largest helicopter in use today (*Brian M. Service*)

MIL
V-12 (Mi-12)

USSR

Known to NATO under the reporting name *Homer*, the V-12 was designed as a heavy general-purpose helicopter with accommodation for military and civil payloads compatible with those of the large Antonov An-22 fixed-wing transport. Although it remained a prototype, and its expected role has been taken over by the new Mil M-26, it remains the largest helicopter ever built.

Its existence was first confirmed in March 1969, when it was announced that it had set a number of payload-to-height records which exceeded by some 20 per cent the records established previously by the Mi-6 and Mi-10K. Flying from an airfield in Moscow on 22 February 1969, the helicopter had climbed at a rate of more than 180 m (600 ft)/min to an altitude of 2,951 m (9,682 ft), carrying a payload of 31,030 kg (68,410 lb). This represented new records for maximum load lifted to an altitude of 2,000 m, and for altitude attained with payloads of 20,000, 25,000, and 30,000 kg. This record was exceeded

Mil V-12 (Mi-12), the largest helicopter ever built (*Brian M. Service*)

on 6 August 1969 when a payload of 40,204.5 kg (88,636 lb) was lifted to an altitude of 2,255 m (7,398 ft).

Work on the V-12 is said to have begun in 1965, the original specification calling for a tandem-rotor configuration, using existing dynamic components. Instead, Mil developed the helicopter with a side-by-side rotor layout. Powered by four 4,847 kW (6,500 shp) Soloviev D-25VF turbo-shaft engines, mounted in pairs under the tips of the fixed wings, each pair was coupled to drive one five-blade rotor. Accommodation was provided for two pilots, a flight engineer and an electrician in the nose cockpit of the fuselage, above which was a smaller cockpit for the navigator and radio operator in tandem. The unobstructed main cargo hold had rails in the roof for an electrically-operated platform-mounted travelling crane, with four loading points each capable of lifting 2,500 kg (5,500 lb) and a maximum capacity of 10,000 kg (22,000 lb) for a single item. About 50 folding seats along the side walls were provided for work crews or troops accompanying freight loads.

The prototype V-12 was reported to have crashed in 1969, mainly as a result of engine failure. Two further prototypes were flying by 1971, when it was expected that the helicopter would go into production. However, it is now known that the V-12 remained a prototype.

Above: Mil V-12 (Mi-12) with its rear clamshell doors opened and loading ramp lowered (*Tass*)

Below: The giant Soviet Myasishchev M-4 reconnaissance bomber (*Bison-C*) on display to the public alongside other warplanes (*Novosti*)

MYASISHCHEV
M-4

USSR

Known to NATO under the reporting name *Bison*, the M-4 was designed as a heavy strategic bomber. It was, in fact, the Soviet Union's first operational four-jet strategic bomber, the design of which began in 1951, work on the prototype beginning in May 1952, and the bomber appearing over Moscow in May 1954.

Comparable with early versions of the US Boeing B-52 Stratofortress, the first version was coded *Bison-A* by NATO. It is powered by 85.3 kN (19,180 lb st) Mikulin AM-3D turbojets, buried in the wing-roots, and is capable of carrying 4,500 kg (10,000 lb) of nuclear or conventional free-fall bombs over ranges of up to 11,250 km (7,000 miles). Defensive armament comprises ten 23 mm cannon in twin-gun turrets in the tail, above the fuselage fore and aft of the wings and under the fuselage fore and aft of the bomb bays, thought necessary as the bomber is believed to have a service ceiling of only 13,700 m (45,000 ft).

About 31 converted *Bison-As* are currently serving as flight refuelling tankers for the 43 remaining M-4 bombers and also the Tu-95 strategic bombers of the Soviet strategic bomber force, carrying a hose-reel unit in the bomb bay. However, only a few of the *Bison-B* and *C* maritime reconnaissance versions remain operational, their role having been taken over by new aircraft of much greater capability. *Bison-B*, like *Bison-C*, has only six guns for defence, with deletion of the after guns above and below the fuselage. It features a 'solid' nose in place of the hemispherical glazed nose of *Bison-A*, with a large superimposed flight refuelling probe. Numerous underfuselage blister fairings house specialised avionic equipment. *Bison-C* is similar to *Bison-B* but can be identified by its longer nose with a central refuelling probe, the nose housing a large search radar. A prone bombing/observation station, with optically-flat glass panels, is featured below and to the rear of the radar, whilst further small windows and a domed observation window are positioned each side of the forward fuselage.

In 1959 a *Bison-C*, carrying the experimental designation 201-M, was used to set up a number of official records. Powered by 127.5 kN (28,660 lb st) Soloviev D-15 turbojet engines, this aircraft established seven payload-to-height records, including a weight of 55,220 kg (121,480 lb) lifted to 2,000 m (6,560 ft) and an altitude of 15,317 m (50,253 ft) with a 10,000 kg payload.

Myasishchev M-4 (Bison-C)

NORTH AMERICAN
XB-70A Valkyrie

USA

There can be little doubt that the XB-70 was the most complex strategic bomber ever built, and certainly the fastest. Intended as a Boeing B-52 Stratofortress replacement, it was a tail-first delta-wing bomber designed to fly the entire distance to and from the target at Mach 3, carrying nuclear or conventional weapons.

The initial USAF requirement for a B-52 replacement was issued as early as October 1954, when it was envisaged that the replacement bomber from whatever manufacturer would cruise at subsonic speeds and 'dash' supersonically. Initial design studies by North American and Boeing indicated that the required payload and range could be achieved only by an aircraft weighing 340,000 kg (750,000 lb) and carrying huge external fuel tanks on jettisonable outer wing panels. However, further study showed that use of a high-energy chemical fuel, combined with the very latest aerodynamic advances (notably compression lift), might make possible a much smaller aircraft which would cruise supersonically throughout the flight.

North American and Boeing submitted new design proposals, and in late 1957 North American was announced the winner. Simultaneously, General Electric was awarded a contract to develop J93-GE-5 turbojet engines to burn chemical fuel. However, it was later decided that these engines and their fuel were an unnecessary complication, and instead six 137.9 kN (31,000 lb

st) J93-GE-3 turbojets would be employed.

Then, on 3 December 1959, the B-70 bomber programme was cut right back following a review of the likely future requirements for manned aircraft. This left an order for just one prototype. Whilst development of the bomber's advanced operational sub-systems was cancelled altogether, an exception was made of the stellar-inertial bombing-navigation system.

In 1960 the B-70 programme was again boosted to include the prototype, a test airframe and twelve operational bombers, as well as renewed development of the sub-systems, but in March 1961 it was once again cut in view of America's forthcoming missile capability. However, to ensure that America retained the necessary technology should it require such a bomber at a later date, three XB-70A aerodynamic research aircraft were funded. In March 1963 this was cut to two.

The XB-70A was first shown in public on 11 May 1964 and the first flight was achieved on 21 September the same year. Mach 1 was exceeded on 12 October 1964 and Mach 3 on 14 October 1965. Altitudes reached during routine flights were around 21,500 m (70,000 ft). The second aircraft flew on 17 July 1965 but was lost on 8 June 1966 when, after a 2¼-hr flight, an F-104 chase aircraft collided with it. By this time the two aircraft had flown 95 times, including more than 81 hours in supersonic flight. The first XB-70A went on to complete 71 flights by 20 February 1968, by which time NASA had taken over management of the programme. The whole XB-70A test programme was terminated in 1969.

The XB-70A incorporated many unique design features, including wingtips which folded down hydraulically to an angle of 25° for low-altitude supersonic flight and to 65° for high-altitude Mach 3 cruising flight (to improve stability and manoeuvrability), twelve trailing-edge elevons and a rectangular-section powerplant duct under the wings.

Right: **North American XB-70A Valkyrie, the fastest bomber ever built**

Below: **Roll-out of the North American XB-70A Valkyrie** (*Robert D. Archer*)

NORTHROP
B-35 and YB-49

USA

The XB-35 and YB-49 were flying-wing bombers, designed and built by Northrop for the USAAF/USAF. Although Germany also researched along similar lines, the nearest this country got to an operational flying-wing aircraft was its Horten Ho IX, which was intended to go into production as the Gotha Go 229 day and night fighter and fighter-bomber. However, the prototypes while still under construction were discovered by the advancing Allied forces at the end of the war.

Northrop began serious flying-wing research with its N-1M, a small experimental aircraft powered by two low-powered piston engines.

Northrop YB-35 flying-wing bomber (*US Air Force*)

This aircraft met the criteria of a flying wing, in that the aircraft had no tail surfaces or fuselage, the crew were accommodated within the contours of the aerofoil, and that no portion of the aircraft did not contribute directly to lift. With the success of the N-1M Northrop submitted a proposal to the USAAF in September 1941 for a full-scale long-range bomber version. Despite its highly unconventional layout, it was decided to proceed with the project. The Wright Field Engineering Division co-operated with Northrop from this point.

Work on the prototype of the full-size bomber, designated XB-35, began in 1943 at Northrop's Hawthorne plant. In the meantime, four N-9M one-third scale flying-wings were built to obtain useful data and familiarise pilots with this type of

Northrop YB-49 turbojet-powered flying-wing bomber (*US Air Force***)**

aircraft. The XB-35 flew for the first time on 25 June 1946. Powered by two Pratt & Whitney R-4360-17 and two R-4360-21 Wasp Major piston engines, each rated at 2,237 kW (3,000 hp) and driving four-blade contra-rotating pusher propellers, it was a 52.43 m (172 ft) span straight-tapered and sweptback wing constructed in one piece. Drag-inducing double-split flaps were fitted at the wingtips for directional control, with elevons between these and the outer engines. Fixed wingtip slots in the leading-edge opened only at speeds approaching the stall. A crew of seven were accommodated in a fuselage nacelle constructed around the centreline of the wing, the pilot being situated in a forward cockpit offset to port with a bubble canopy. Defensive arma-ment comprised two electrically-operated four-gun turrets, one above and one below the wing, and four electrically-operated remotely-control-led two-gun turrets, one above and one below each outer wing section.

Following extensive trials, fourteen service test YB-35s were ordered for the USAF, two of which were later reassigned as YB-49 prototypes. The first YB-49 flew on 21 October 1947. It was basically similar to the YB-35 but was powered by eight 17.8 kN (4,000 lb st) Allison J-35 turbojet engines. So successful were the YB-35s and YB-49s that in 1948 thirty production B-49 bombers were ordered for service with the USAF. However, in the following year these were cancelled. A six-jet reconnaissance-bomber ver-sion of the YB-49 was also built and flown, and projected derivatives of the YB-49 included a commercial airliner.

PENHOËT
Flying-Boat

Penhoët flying-boat

France

Chantier et Ateliers de St-Nazaire (Penhoët) was a famous French dockyard which conducted extensive experiments with catapults, a successful model being installed on French light cruisers. Among other activities, Penhoët produced a giant flying-boat, which first flew at Loire on 26 June 1926, piloted by M. Duhamel.

Designed by M. Richard, the flying-boat had biconvex-section cantilever monoplane wings of steel reinforced wooden construction, which varied in thickness from 1.8 m (7 ft) at the roots to 1 m (3 ft 3 in) at the tips, and in chord from 9 m (29 ft 7 in) at the roots to 5 m (16 ft 5 in) at the tips. Large stabilising floats were fitted under the wings. Power was provided by five 313 kW (420 hp) Gnome-Rhône-built Bristol Jupiter engines, two in each wing leading-edge and one in the upper hull. The hull itself was a single-step type of wooden construction, with a maximum depth of 3.8 m (12ft 5½ in).

Flight trials of the giant began with a number of successful alightings with the engines on. However, on 1 July an attempt was made to alight with the engines throttled right back. As a result the pilot was unable to flatten out properly and the bow of the flying-boat drove into the water, causing damage to the fore part of the hull. Little more was heard of the flying-boat.

PIASECKI
PV-15 Transporter

USA

The Transporter was a very large experimental transport helicopter, two of which were ordered by the USAF in mid-1949. The first was military designated YH-16 and was the dynamic test vehicle, powered by two 1,230 kW (1,650 hp) Pratt & Whitney R-2180-11 engines. This helicopter first flew on 23 October 1953, but proved to be underpowered.

The second helicopter was the YH-16A, powered by two Allison T38-A-6 turboshaft engines of nearly 2,237 kW (3,000 shp) each. It appeared in 1954 and pre-flight tethered testing had been completed by the spring of 1955. Flight testing proper was then expected to begin, but the Transporter remained a prototype. Plans also called for the YH-16 to be re-engined with Allison T56 turboshafts as the YH-16B.

The Transporter had normal accommodation for a crew of three and 40 passengers. However, alternative layouts allowed for 32 stretchers and attendants or freight, a ramp under the upswept rear fuselage providing easy access to the hold.

Piasecki YH-16 Transporter

R101
Airship

German Zeppelin airships, used in maritime patrol and long-range bombing roles during the First World War, had demonstrated that it should be possible to build large commercial airships to provide intercontinental passenger services. Britain emerged from the war with a small number of indifferent rigid airships, but the RAF was looking forward to the entry into service of two new vessels: the R33 and R34. The latter gained fame, for between 2 and 6 July 1919, it accomplished the first crossing of the North Atlantic by an airship. When the R34 returned to its base at Pulham, Norfolk, airship enthusiasts were armed with convincing proof that here, indeed, was the vehicle needed to establish vital links between the home country and its widely spread empire.

Typically, not a great deal happened for some time. Then, in 1921, the airship branch of the RAF was broken up, the government deciding that the Department of Civil Aviation would look after airships and their development. It was planned that government airships would be operated for commercial users, leading to the strange sight of the R33 and R36 being used in 1921 for traffic control during major race meetings at Epsom and Ascot respectively. It took two more years to decide to promote a programme of airship development, with a sum of £1.3 million allocated for the purpose. In due course the design of two intercontinental-range passenger-carrying airships was sponsored: the R100 and R101. The first was built by private enterprise at Howden, Yorkshire. The slightly larger R101, 220.68 m (724 ft) in length, was built by a government establishment, the Royal Airship Works at Cardington, Bedfordshire.

Construction of the R100 proceeded steadily, and was to result in a practical and workmanlike vessel. The R101, however, has been a subject of controversy for many years. Contemporary reports regard it as a pinnacle of design achievement, or condemn it as a thoughtless botch-up. It introduced steel tube into airship structures: promotional statistics claim that 43.5 km (27 miles) of steel (about 25 per cent) and duralumin tube were involved. It was designed to carry 100 passengers, with accommodation on two decks.

The upper included a main saloon, measuring 18.29 by 9.75 m (60 by 32 ft), plus a dining room to accommodate 50 at a sitting, passengers' sleeping berths, and toilet/washroom facilities. Below was a smokers' lounge, additional sleeping berths, and the living and sleeping quarters for the crew.

It was not until 14 October 1929 that the R101 was able to make its maiden flight, some two months ahead of the R100. During November a number of trial flights were made, the longest a circular tour of 30 hours 35 minutes duration that took in Belfast and Edinburgh as turning points. A passenger on one of these flights, made in fair weather, wrote to *The Times*: '. . . the airship is steadier than the train; quieter than the aeroplane; less given to rolling than sea-going ships. She has all the virtues of these three, and others of her own. . . Her movements are deliberate, her progress serene'. Quite clearly, all was well with the government's creation. Or was it?

The first sour note came from an Air Ministry announcement, late in 1929, that lift of the R101 was to be increased by the insertion of a new mid-section, complete with extra gasbag. A little later one learned that equipment was being removed to reduce weight. More startling, perhaps, buoyancy was being lost, probably from leaking gas valves. Apparently nothing was done. Then, in late August, it was announced that the new bay and its gas bag had been inserted. No comment was made of the fact that passenger capacity had been reduced from 100 to 52, and that the ship was still losing gas.

Knowing these facts, it seems almost unbelievable that on the evening of 4 October 1930, she set out on a voyage to India, with a total of 54 persons on board. Within a few hours the R101 had struck the ground, near Beauvais, France, being totally destroyed by fire. Only eight of those on board survived: the dead were brought home to lie in state in Westminster Abbey before being buried with full military honours at Cardington. With them were buried a host of unanswered questions, and without answers, then or later, airship development in Britain was also buried.

R101, the largest airship built in the United Kingdom

ROCKWELL INTERNATIONAL B-1

USA

Despite the cancellation of the XB-70 Valkyrie, as described under that heading, studies into a B-52 replacement started again in 1962, leading to the AMSA (Advanced Manned Strategic Aircraft) requirement of 1965 for a low-altitude penetration bomber. In 1969 the Department of Defense requested proposals from manufacturers and in mid-1970 it awarded North American Rockwell's Los Angeles Division research, development, test and evaluation contracts and General Electric a contract for the F101 engine. Originally it was intended to build five flying prototypes, two structural test airframes and 40 engines, but in early 1971 these quantities were reduced to three flying prototypes, one ground test aircraft and 27 engines. Later a fourth flying aircraft was added. At this time it was intended that the USAF would receive 244 B-1s.

The first B-1 flew for the first time on 23 December 1974, and by February 1977 the three flight test aircraft had flown 88 times, reaching by then a maximum speed of Mach 2.1. However, on 30 June 1977 B-1 production was cancelled by President Carter in favour of cruise missile development, although continued testing and development of the B-1 prototypes was authorised.

The fourth B-1 flew on 14 February 1979,

Rockwell International B-1

representing an operational configuration, with both defensive and offensive avionics systems installed. Meanwhile, as a result of the cruise missile programme, the Department of Defense looked for a suitable aircraft to carry the airborne version of the missile, with the result that in 1979 initial planning was made for a derivative version of the B-1 as a strategic ALCM launcher. It was decided that the third prototype would be modified to this configuration and work on it began in 1980. The SAL (Strategic ALCM Launcher) was then scheduled to fly for the first time in 1981. In the same year President Reagan requested authority to purchase for the USAF a total of 100 SALs (B-1Bs), for operational deployment from 1985.

Designed to operate at treetop heights at near-sonic speed, and at supersonic speeds at high altitude, the B-1 as originally designed has a radar signature about 5 per cent as large as that of the B-52. The SAL derivative is likely to include the latest design innovations, including spin-off from the stealth programmes. It is a variable-geometry bomber, powered by four 133.4 kN (30,000 lb st) with afterburning General Electric F101-GE-100 turbofan engines, mounted in pairs beneath the fixed centre-section of the wing. As originally planned it would have carried up to 24 SRAM missiles in three bomb bays or up to 34,020 kg (75,000 lb) of nuclear or conventional bombs. In SAL form it will carry ALCMs (Air Launched Cruise Missiles), and its performance may be reduced from that first planned by the deletion of certain design features, such as the VG inlets, although the performance figures quoted on the tables are for the aircraft with the VG inlets.

SAUNDERS-ROE
Princess

UK

In 1943 Saunders-Roe began preliminary studies for an extremely large flying-boat, and in July 1945 the Ministry of Supply invited the company to tender for the construction of such an aircraft. Authorisation was given in the following May for three prototypes, BOAC having already shown interest in using the 105-220-seat 'double-bubble'-hull type on a direct London to New York service. But BOAC interest was short-lived, as it became clear that the flying-boat era was well and truly over and that modern landplanes could safely complete the journey non-stop at lower overall cost. And so, in early 1951, BOAC withdrew its support.

The Saunders-Roe Princess prior to its launch

But, even with this setback, it was clear that the Princess, as the flying-boat had been named, had great potential as a bulk carrier, and so the prototypes were designated as long-range military transports for the RAF. However, in March 1952 it was announced that only the first Princess would be completed immediately, powered by ten 2,819 kW (3,780 shp) Bristol Proteus 600 Series turboprop engines, while the remaining two would await the availability of the Proteus 705s. The engines themselves were in four coupled pairs and two single units, the coupled engines driving two contra-rotating propellers.

The first Princess flew for the first time on 22 August 1952, and was flown in civil guise with the registration G-ALUN. In the following year it was confirmed that flight trials with this flying-boat, to include pressurised flights at an altitude of 9,150 m (30,000 ft), were to proceed to a total of 100 flying hours. The preliminary programme was completed in 1954, when it was decided to suspend further flying until the later engines became available. But this actually spelt the end of the Princess. The second Princess was never flown and the third was not completed.

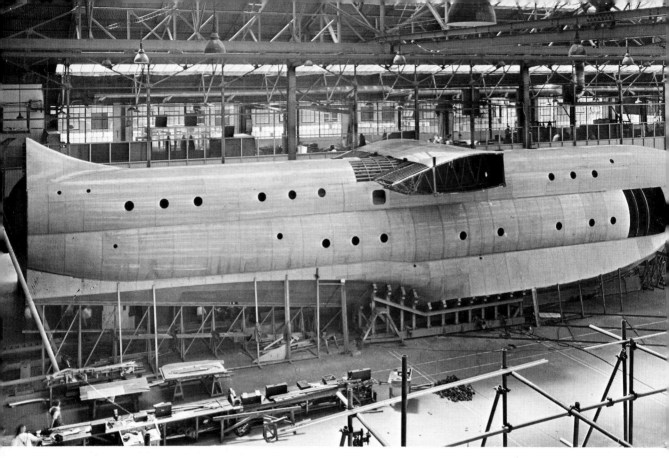

Above: Saunders-Roe Princess hull under construction   **Below:** Rear view of the giant Princess flying-boat

Saunders-Roe Princess flying-boat at a Farnborough air display (*RAF Museum, Hendon*)

SHIN MEIWA
SS-2 and SS-2A

Japan

The largest flying-boat in use today, the SS-2 was developed as an anti-submarine flying-boat with STOL performance for the Japan Maritime Self-Defence Force. This version received the JMSDF designation PS-1. A search and rescue amphibious derivative followed as the SS-2A, JMSDF-designated US-1.

The first PS-1 prototype took to the air on 5 October 1967 and the second in mid-1968, and both were delivered to the 51st Flight Test Squadron at Iwakuni. As a result the PS-1 was ordered into production, and by 1981 23 had been delivered. Designed to dip its large sonar into the sea during many landings and take-offs, the PS-1 can land on very rough water, in winds of up to 47 km/h (29 mph). Take-offs and landings have been made successfully in seas with wave heights of up to 3 m (10 ft). To resist salt-water corrosion, much of the structure uses special alloys, coated with a watertight polyurethane compound developed by Shin Meiwa. Accommodation is provided for two pilots and a flight engineer on the flight deck, to the rear of which is a tactical compartment housing two sonar operators, a navigator, magnetic anomaly detector (MAD) operator, radar operator, radio operator and a tactical co-ordinator. Electronic, magnetic and sonic equipment is installed on the starboard side, with the crew's rest area and bunks on the port side. Aft of the tactical compartment is the weapons compartment with 20 sonobuoys, Julie active acoustic echo ranging with 12 explosive charges, four 330 lb anti-submarine bombs, and smoke bombs. Externally-carried armament includes an underwing pod between each pair of engine nacelles, each containing two homing torpedoes, and a launcher beneath each wingtip for three 5 in air-to-surface rockets. Power is provided by four 2,282 kW (3,060 ehp) Ishikawa-jima-built General Electric T64-IHI-10 turboprop engines. In addition, a T58-IHI-10 gas turbine is housed in the upper centre portion of the fuselage to provide power for the boundary layer control system on the rudder, flaps and elevators, which enhances control and stability in low-speed flight.

Design of the US-1 air/sea rescue amphibian began in 1970 and take-off was achieved on 16 October 1974. Four had been delivered to the JMSDF by the spring of 1980, when four more had been funded.

Shin Meiwa has also developed a water bomber version of the PS-1, in co-operation with the JMSDF and the National Fire Agency. The prototype for testing was the converted first PS-1 prototype. Water tanks of 8.1 tons capacity have been tested, but plans call for an eventual 14 ton water capacity. The proposed production version could deliver 315 tonnes (310 tons) of water, picked up at 70 km (43.5 miles) from its base, to a site 10 km (6 miles) away before needing to refuel.

Shin Meiwa US-1 amphibious flying-boat

SHORT
Cromarty

UK

During the First World War Short Brothers earned a considerable reputation as a manufacturer of successful torpedo-bombing and reconnaissance seaplanes. Perhaps the best known of these was the Short 184, a single-engined biplane that was responsible in 1915 for sinking the first ship with an air-launched torpedo. In the final few months of war Short Brothers also completed examples of the Felixstowe F.3 flying-boat, thereafter producing improved F.5s. This unremarkable move to flying-boat construction was to have profound repercussions on the future employment of the company.

Work on the F.3s had given Short Brothers a grounding in the construction of large flying-boats, and eventually the company introduced refinements to the F.5 which actually improved sea-going qualities. But, before this, Short Brothers had submitted a design to the Admiralty for a new flying-boat for use with the Fast Cruiser Squadron. Both Short Brothers and Vickers were selected to produce three prototypes each of their aircraft, but the end of the war took the urgency out of construction. Work on the Short aircraft began in early 1919 and the first Cromarty, as it became known, flew on 19 April 1921. The pilot was J.B. Parker, formerly Assistant-Paymaster, Royal Navy. He had been one of the best pilots to serve with the RNAS before being invalided out. Parker had then been appointed to manage the London office of Short Brothers, which had its main works at Rochester, Kent.

The Cromarty itself was heavily influenced by the F.3 configuration, and had been designed to not only take off and alight in rough water but to be able to be moored out in only slightly protected harbours. The latter feature was essential for a flying-boat that was to be flown great distances, economising greatly in shed accommodation and handling by groundcrew at its stations. Powered by two Rolls-Royce Condor engines, installed between the unequal-span wings, the aircraft's hull was basically a spruce structure with a plywood skin. One of its main differences to the F.3 was the use of a biplane-type tail unit with auxiliary rudders flanking the large central fin and rudder. Pilot and co-pilot were accommodated side-by-side in a cockpit forward of the wings, while the gunner/bombardier was situated in the bow and was to have operated a 37 mm automatic anti-submarine gun.

Before the second Cromarty had been completed, the number of prototypes ordered was reduced to one from each company. The Vickers Valentia had been assembled at Barrow, although the hull was constructed at Cowes. In mid-1922 this crashed, so ending the Valentia's chances of orders. Meanwhile, the Cromarty had been continually revised. Eventually the newly installed higher-rated 485 kW (650 hp) Condor engines with Valentia four-blade propellers provided the performance required, and official reports from the Seaplane Development Flight looked encouraging. However, in 1922 the Cromarty was severely damaged by a reef while being taxied, and was beached in the Scilly Isles. Nothing could be done economically to save this first Short flying-boat, and it was scrapped. A commercial passenger-carrying version had also been planned, with special attention to overall comfort: the passenger cabin was to have been heated and the engines silenced as much as possible. Although this did not progress beyond the design stage, the Cromarty experience left Short Brothers with a clearer idea of what constituted an efficient flying-boat, experience that was to serve the company well throughout the interwar period.

Short Cromarty

SHORT
Kent

UK

The type name Kent applied to three flying-boats built for Imperial Airways, named *Scipio*, *Sylvanus* and *Satyrus*. Need for these new four-engined long-range flying-boats arose from the difficulty Imperial Airways was having in operating its new London to India service, begun in March 1929. Italy refused to allow Imperial Airways aircraft flying via France to use Italian ports from 31 October that year, as Italy wanted to share the revenue from the Genoa-Alexandria route, which meant that the Argosy biplane and train route to Genoa had to be rethought. Imperial got around the problem by linking Paris with Salonika, Greece, where the Calcutta flying-boat took over the route to Alexandria. But the air route to Alexandria included a stop to refuel at Tobruk. Without this stop the Mirabella, Crete, to Alexandria stage was beyond the range of the Calcutta. Other options were examined, but in the end it was decided that the only answer was to operate flying-boats that could fly non-stop between Mirabella and Alexandria.

For this service Short designed its Kent class, basically a fifteen-passenger and four-engined scaled-up Calcutta. Interestingly, virtually as soon as the flying-boats were ready for service, an Italian change of heart meant that Imperial was able to rethink its European sections of the London-India service and adopted a train journey between Basle and Genoa, from where a Calcutta took over. Then, in October 1931, Imperial again modified its train routes for the London to Cairo service to include journeys between Paris and Brindisi and Alexandria and Cairo, a service which was now independent of the India route from Athens and carried on to Mwanza, later to be extended to Cape Town.

The first Kent, named *Scipio* by Imperial Airways, first flew on 24 February 1931, followed in March and April by the launchings of *Sylvanus* and *Satyrus* respectively. The expected arrival of the Kents gave Imperial the chance of using the smaller Calcuttas on the Khartoum, Kosti, Malakal, Juba, Kampala and Kisumu sectors of the London to Mwanza service. On 16 May 1931, *Satyrus* inaugurated Kent services from Genoa, while *Scipio* departed Alexandria on the India route. Within a short time *Scipio* and *Sylvanus* had

been damaged, causing great strain on the Calcuttas, which had to cope temporarily with both routes. However, when the Kents returned they operated several routes without major incident until *Sylvanus* and *Scipio* were put out of action by sabotage in 1935 and a heavy landing in 1936 respectively. *Satyrus* was retired in 1938.

The Kent itself was an unequal-span biplane flying-boat, with four 447 kW (600 hp) Bristol Jupiter XF.BM radial engines mounted in monocoque nacelles and supported by vertical duralumin tube struts between the wings. The hull was a standard Short two-step structure, covered above the water-line by anodically-treated duralumin and under by stainless steel, so that the boat could be moored out for long periods without risk of deterioration. Accommodation in the main cabin was for fifteen passengers, their journey being eased by large windows, sound-insulated walls, good ventilation, lighting and heating, a toilet and wash-room facilities, and a completely equipped steward's compartment. A compartment for 9.9 m³ (350 cu ft) of baggage, mail or freight was provided.

Below: Short Kent
Right: Short Scylla, basically a landplane version of the Kent for Imperial Airways. Two built

SHORT-MAYO
Composite

UK

The first non-stop crossing of the North Atlantic (West-East) had been achieved by a Vickers Vimy bomber in 1919, and in the years that followed there were a number of other successful pioneering flights over this route. Despite these achievements, by the mid-1930s it had not proved possible to establish a commercial air service linking Britain and the United States. A West-East crossing posed the least problems: one from East-West, against the prevailing winds, represented a challenge that could not then be met. At that time, aviation technology was insufficiently advanced to cover the design and development of aircraft with adequate range and payload capability for operation over such a route. If passengers were to be carried safely and punctually, quite large margins of range were needed, allied to reliable multi-engined powerplant installations. In the meantime, a considerable amount of work was done to establish services for the carriage of mail.

It had long been appreciated that an aircraft could fly quite safely, and remain airborne, at a gross weight considerably higher than that at which it could take off under its own power. An engineer's practical understanding of this point led to the design and construction in Britain of a fascinating composite aircraft. The concept, which was thought out and developed by Major R.H. Mayo, involved the use of a large aircraft to carry a small heavily-laden machine into the air. At a suitable operating height, the upper component would be released, continuing in flight to its destination while the launching aircraft returned to base.

This idea appealed to the British Air Ministry, and Short Bros at Rochester was contracted to build a prototype, named as the Mayo Composite Aircraft. This consisted of a lower (launching) aircraft, later named *Maia*, virtually a standard four-engined Short 'Empire'-type flying-boat. It differed by having wings of increased span, and had support structure for the upper component above the wings and hull. Later named *Mercury*, the upper component was a considerably smaller floatplane of cantilever high-wing monoplane configuration. Powered by four 682 kW (915 hp) Bristol Pegasus X radial engines, it had accommo-

dation for a crew of two and approximately 454 kg (1,000 lb) of cargo.

The prototype combination was completed towards the end of 1937, and after individual and combined testing, the first flight with separation of the two components was made successfully on 6 February 1938. Both aircraft were able to operate independently of each other, but at its maximum loaded weight the *Mercury* could become airborne only if launched by *Maia*. Shortly after completion of testing, the two aircraft were handed over to Imperial Airways for experimental operations over the North Atlantic.

The first mail-carrying transatlantic flight was made on 21-22 July 1938, *Mercury* piloted by Captain D.C.T. Bennet separating from *Maia* near Foynes, and flying non-stop to Montreal carrying a full payload of mail and newspapers. This represented the first heavier-than-air commercial crossing of the North Atlantic. After partial refuelling at Montreal, *Mercury* took off under its own power and continued to New York. The return flight, via Botwood, the Azores, and Lisbon, was accomplished successfully during 25-27 July. Subsequently, following launch by *Maia* at Dundee on 6 October 1938, and again piloted by Captain Bennet, *Mercury* established a world long-distance record for seaplanes of 9,652 km (5,997.5 miles), landing on the Orange River, South Africa, after a non-stop flight of 42 hours 5 minutes. The return journey was accomplished successfully in stages.

Despite such promising performance, no further transatlantic trials could be conducted during the winter months, since Botwood would be icebound. Then, with the coming of the summer of 1939, the gathering war clouds in Europe brought an end to further experiments. *Maia* was destroyed by enemy bombs during May 1941, and *Mercury* was scrapped only three months later.

Above right: Short-Mayo Composite

Right: Maia and *Mercury* separate on 21 July 1938, the beginning of *Mercury's* flight to Montreal

SHORT
Sarafand

UK

Construction of the Cromarty heralded for Short Brothers a line of successful flying-boats that, by the late 1920s, included the Singapore and Calcutta. Oswald Short's predilection for large flying-boats had, in the event, proved to be technically and financially feasible. But even Oswald's experience, and that of Short's designers, was going to be stretched to the limit with the latest project, later named the Sarafand.

Although Germany's giant Dornier Do X was viewed in 1929 as a truly magnificent flying-boat, its twelve engines, vast wing span and generous accommodation hid poor hydrodynamic design. Indeed, the Do X had the greatest difficulty reaching New York on its subsequent transatlantic flight. In the meantime, Oswald Short produced a design for what was basically a scaled-up Singapore, powered by six engines. However, the Short flying-boat was to be a military type, its range being sufficient for transatlantic and empire flights.

Eventually the Air Ministry decided to partially fund a prototype and issued Specification R.6/28. When eventually completed, the Sarafand was the world's second largest aeroplane, although with more horsepower than the larger Do X. Designed for patrol, reconnaissance and liaison duties, it was an equal-span biplane of remarkable design. The upper wing was supported by struts from the engine nacelles and two pairs of vertical interplane struts. The wing structure consisted of two stainless steel spars, standard Short-type tubular duralumin ribs, large diameter drag-struts made from pressed-up duralumin sheet picking up the top and bottom spar booms and tie-rod bracing, all fabric-covered. Walkways were provided on the lower wings, where necessary. The hull was a two-step structure, originally with a stainless steel bottom so that it could be moored out for long periods without risk of deterioration, but subsequently of duralumin and Alclad. The six 615 kW (825 hp) Rolls-Royce Buzzard IIIMS engines were mounted in tandem pairs in monocoque nacelles midway between the wings, fed from four fuel tanks in the upper wing and two overload tanks in the lower wings. Normal accommodation was for a crew of ten. The bow cockpit had either a Lewis gun or a 1½-pdr

automatic gun, bomb-aimer's position and marine gear. The totally enclosed pilots' cockpit had seating for two in tandem, with dual controls, below which was a passage-way to the ward room which housed the wireless, navigator's chart board and the engineer's control panels. A compartment between the spar frames was to be used as officers' quarters, incorporating four folding bunks and a removable table. The crew quarters followed, with another compartment for bunks, stretcher stowage and equipment maintenance thereafter. Midships gun rings were staggered, and aft of these positions was a toilet. A walkway to the extreme tail gave access to the tail gun position. Equipment on board the Sarafand included telephone intercommunication linking up nine positions in the hull.

The Sarafand made its first flight on 30 June 1932 and in July it was demonstrated to an excited Press. It was handed over to the RAF soon after, with whom it remained an experimental type until being retired in 1936.

Below: **Short Sarafand**   *Right:* **Short Sarafand**

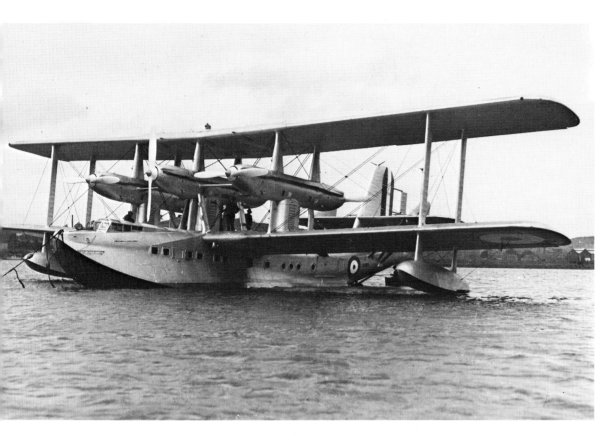

SHORT
Shetland

_UK_

The Shetland was a very large flying-boat, designed to Specification R.14/40 as a long-range reconnaissance type for the RAF to supersede the Sunderland. Design work began in 1940, but before completion of the first prototype its role was changed as a result of official policy. It was subsequently intended as an unarmed military transport, and in this form the prototype Shetland flew for the first time on 14 December 1944, from the Medway. As certain military features had already been incorporated, these were faired over with smooth metal sheet. However, once again the role of the Shetland was revised, this time making it a purely commercial aircraft.

Unfortunately, on 28 January 1946 it was accidently destroyed by fire while moored at Felixstowe.

A second prototype was built from the start as a commercial flying-boat, known as the Shetland II. This was launched at Rochester on 15 September 1947 and flew for the first time two days later. Externally, this was identifiable by its more rounded nose and pointed tailcone, both resulting from the omission of gun positions as expected to be fitted on the original Shetland. Accommodation was arranged on two decks. The flight compartment, on the upper deck forward of the leading-edge of the wings, accommodated two pilots, a navigator, radio operator and flight

Military configured Short Shetland I

engineer. On the port side of the compartment was a stairway leading to the lower deck. Behind this stairway was a settee, convertible to two bunks, for off-duty crew. Continuing along the upper deck were the auxiliary engine room, the main mail compartment, a fully equipped kitchen, dining saloon or lounge for twelve, and cocktail bar. From the bar was a staircase leading down to the rear entry vestibule on the lower deck. The Purser's office was below the stairway. Opposite the stairway was a coat room and to the rear a men's dressing room. In the extreme tail was stowage space for baggage. Above the dressing room was a second mail or freight compartment. Going forward from the vestibule along the lower deck were four passenger cabins, each seating two and convertible into two-berth sleeping cabins, four toilets, eight passenger cabins for four persons each or convertible into two-berth cabins, and the forward entrance vestibule, at the sides of which were a ladies' toilet and dressing room. This layout allowed for the carriage of 40 passengers and mail or freight, but in fact the Shetland II could have accommodated up to 70 passengers.

Power for the Shetland II was provided by four 1,864 kW (2,500 hp) Bristol Centaurus radial engines, each driving a D.H. Hydromatic four-blade constant-speed full-feathering propeller. Total fuel capacity was 27,785 litres (6,112 Imp gallons). However, despite its potential, BOAC neither wanted this flying-boat for use on its regular services nor any production examples, and so it was designated an engine testbed. This bogus role was officially ended in 1951, when the giant was reduced to scrap.

Short Shetland II (*Flight*)

Short Shetland I

SHORT
Belfast

UK

It is difficult when looking at the Belfast to believe that its design was originally based upon the Bristol Britannia, but this was indeed the case. However, the finished aeroplane had little in common with the airliner. For a start it was developed specifically for carrying heavy freight, including the largest guns, vehicles, missiles and other equipment used by the RAF and British Army, although by simple conversion 150-250 troops could have been carried (the larger number with use of a removable upper floor). The Belfast also incorporated 'beaver-tail' rear loading doors so that military vehicles could be driven straight into the hold, in addition to a large door on one side of the fuselage.

Intended for military and commercial use, the Belfast was only built for the RAF, which received a total of ten. Powered by four 4,270 kW (5,730 ehp) Rolls-Royce Tyne RTy.12 turboprop engines, the first example flew on 5 January 1964, construction having begun in October 1959. The second flew on 1 May the same year. As the

Belfast C.Mk 1, the ten aircraft entered service with No 53 Squadron, RAF, from January 1966, remaining operational until 1976, when they were phased out of service as part of a programme of defence cuts. This left the RAF with no heavy freighters, a situation which remains today.

As mentioned above, a commercial counterpart of the RAF's Belfast was projected, together with an improved performance version and a jet-powered development with Rolls-Royce RB.178 by-pass turbojet engines married to a C-141A StarLifter-type wing. None of these progressed past the project stage. However, ex-RAF Belfasts were offered for sale to commercial operators and Pan-African Air Freight-Liners expressed interest in purchasing the entire fleet. However, the major operator of Belfasts is the British airline Heavy Lift Cargo Airlines, based at London's Stansted airport, which currently uses three (others are in reserve).

Right: Unloading a Saladin armoured car, an Abbot 105 mm self-propelled gun and a Ferret scout car from an RAF Short Belfast

Short Belfast in RAF service

191

Short Belfast in the livery of Heavy Lift Cargo Airlines

SIEMENS-SCHUCKERT
R.I to R.VII

Germany

The aviation branch of Siemens-Schuckert, a very large electrical firm, began with the construction of an experimental airship some years before the outbreak of the First World War. When war began, it was the second firm in Germany to take up building giant bombers, beaten only by Zeppelin. The first two giants were started in 1914. The first of these, designed by Forsman in December 1914 and completed in early 1915, was virtually a copy of the Russian Sikorsky biplane and was powered by four Mercedes engines mounted on the lower wings. However, this aircraft was not a success, as it proved to be badly underpowered.

The second giant, designed by Steffen, had three centrally-mounted 112 kW (150 hp) Benz Bz. III engines inside the fuselage, which drove

through an automatic disengaging clutch to a main gear in case one engine failed. From the main gear, universally jointed transmission shafts led to reduction gears for two large propellers. This engine arrangement was common in German experimental R-type heavy bombers. This aircraft became the R.I. Seven aircraft of the series in total were built up to 1917 with various engine installations, the most common being 164 kW (220 hp) Benz Bz. IVs, although 194 kW (260 hp) Mercedes D.IVas were used.

Four Benz-powered R-types were operated on the Eastern Front and the remaining three became trainers.

Right: **Siemens-Schuckert R.VIII, a giant bomber with six 224 kW (300 hp) Basse and Selve BuS IV engines mounted in the fuselage and driving four large propellers, which followed the R.I to R.VII series. Design and construction began at the end of 1917 and the single example built never flew**

Below: **Siemens-Schuckert R.I** (*Imperial War Museum*)

SIKORSKY
Le Grand
and
Ilya Mourometz

Russia

The *Le Grand*, officially-named *Russian Knight*, was the world's first four-engined aeroplane and the first aeroplane with enclosed accommodation for the crew and passengers. However, for such a large aircraft it is perhaps surprising that only four passengers were accommodated, having the use of a sofa, table and wash room.

Powered by four 74.5 kW (100 hp) Argus engines mounted on the lower wings, *Le Grand* flew for the first time on 13 May 1913, Igor Sikorsky himself piloting the aircraft on this ten-minute flight. So successful was this aircraft that 53 flights were made without major problem before it was destroyed on the ground by an engine which fell from an aeroplane flying over it. This tragic event for *Le Grand* marked only the end of the beginning for Sikorsky and giant aircraft, as he had proved his capability as a designer and

Sikorsky *Le Grand* in 1913

pilot. Indeed, on 2 August 1913 the *Le Grand* had managed a flight of 1 hour 54 minutes while carrying eight passengers.

The *Le Grand* had not been Sikorksy's first aircraft by any means, and it is interesting to note that in the November 1912 military trials, Sikorsky took first place ahead of Haber in a Maurice Farman and Boutmy in a Nieuport. However, from *Le Grand* Sikorsky developed the *Ilya Mourometz*. Although it first appeared with a passenger cabin, and it was not unheard of for passengers to promenade along the top of the fuselage while the aircraft was in flight, the *Ilya Mourometz* is best remembered as a bomber.

Indeed, it was the world's first four-engined bomber to become operational. The prototype *Ilya Mourometz* was first flown in January 1914 and in February set up a world height-with-payload record by carrying 16 persons to an altitude of 2,000 m (6,560 ft). Subsequent examples differed slightly, but in total between 70 and 80 were used successfully as bombers during the First World War, the Type B being powered by two 149 kW (200 hp) and two 100.6 kW (135 hp) Salmson-built Canton-Unné engines.

Sikorsky *Ilya Mourometz*

Sikorsky *Ilya Mourometz*

SIKORSKY
1917

SIKORSKY
S-42

USA

Having emigrated to the United States, the Russian aviation engineer Igor Sikorsky formed there his Sikorsky Aero Engineering Corporation on 5 March 1923. It was a difficult time in which to establish a new aircraft manufacturing company, apart from the fact that it was in a new country, but perseverence allied to engineering genius was soon to bring success. Although today the name Sikorsky is associated immediately with rotary-wing aircraft, the company made a significant contribution to aviation history as early as the 1930s, resulting from a series of outstanding amphibians and flying-boats designed by Sikorsky. His S-42 flying-boat, first flown in early 1934, was to record some giant pioneering achievements.

Design of this aircraft was initiated to meet the requirements of Pan American Airways System. As early as the beginning of the 1930s, this US airline was looking out across the oceans that encompassed the nation. To the east lay the North Atlantic, potentially a lucrative route linking the Americas and Europe, but one made difficult by constantly-changing weather con-

ditions. To the west were the vast reaches of the Pacific Ocean, the long ranges that were involved making even pioneering flights a hazardous undertaking. Pan Am decided that the first step was to procure a large, long-range flying-boat, with which to make survey flights of prospective routes, and Sikorsky was given the task of designing and building three examples of this important aircraft.

In configuration it was a braced parasol-wing monoplane, the centre-section of the wing supported by a faired superstructure on top of the hull. The wing incorporated wide-span trailing-edge flaps, and stabilising floats were strut-mounted beneath each wing. A long two-step hull, of all-metal construction, was upswept at the rear, mounting a braced tail unit, comprising a wide-span tailplane and elevators that carried twin fins and rudders on the upper surface. Power for the S-42 was provided by four 522 kW (700 hp) Pratt & Whitney Hornet radial engines, mounted in nacelles at the wing leading-edge, and each driving a variable-pitch propeller. A flight deck and separate main cabin provided accommodation for a crew of six and up to 32 passengers, but for very long-range flights the fuel requirement could reduce the passenger load to as few as eight.

Sikorsky S-42

While construction was proceeding, Pan Am had planned a trans-Pacific route, leading from Alameda, California, via the Pacific islands of Hawaii, Midway, Wake, Guam, and the Philippines to Canton, China. It was a route covering approximately 13,680 km (8,500 miles), and of which the first stage was the longest (3,862 km; 2,400 miles), between Alameda and Honolulu, Hawaii. A surface vessel was sent ahead to make preparations, and by the time that the S-42 had flown for the first time, in March 1934, the planning stage of the operation was complete. Early testing was entirely successful, and the second S-42 (NR-823M) was flown to San Francisco in early 1935 to prepare for the first great stride, Honolulu and return.

Piloted by Captain Edwin C. Musick, with a crew of six, and several bags of mail, the giant flying-boat left Alameda exactly on schedule, at 15.50 hours on 16 April 1935, landing at Honolulu 17 hours 45 minutes later after a completely uneventful crossing. The return journey, flown on 22/23 April, took just on 20 hours. It, too, was completed exactly as planned, and a highly satisfied Captain Musick was to comment that the only thrill was that this important survey flight had been accomplished without unnecessary

thrills. Throughout that year, Captain Musick and his crew became accustomed to the Pacific and the reliability of NR-823M. Round trips were flown to Midway in June, Wake in August, Guam in October, and Manila in early November. The final stage, to Canton, needed the completion of international negotiations before it could be flown. Finally, between 22 November and 6 December 1935, this time flying the Martin M-130 China Clipper (q.v.), Captain Musick and his crew made the first complete trans-Pacific airmail flight, Alameda to Manila and return.

The three S-42s were to be followed by three S-42-As, with 559 kW (750 hp) Pratt & Whitney Hornets and modifications that made it possible to easily convert the standard day cabin to a 14-berth 'sleeper'. Finally, four S-42-Bs were built, introducing aerodynamic improvements and constant-speed propellers. It was one of these S-42-Bs, again piloted by Captain Musick, that was used in March 1937 to survey a Pacific route between the US and New Zealand. Five months later, in August 1937, another of the S-42-Bs surveyed transatlantic routes, travelling outward from New York to Bermuda, the Azores, and Lisbon to Southampton. The return trip was made via Foynes and Botwood. With the accomplishment of such pioneering flights, it is not surprising that the Sikorsky S-42 has an honoured place in aviation history.

Overleaf: Sikorsky S-42

SNCASE
S.E.2010 Armagnac

France

In January 1949 the prototype S.E.2010 Armagnac appeared, a giant airliner with pressurised and soundproofed accommodation for an expected 84, 107 or 160 passengers according to layout. It had been developed from the projected S.E.2000, which had been proposed during the Second World War but had been abandoned at an early stage. Apart from its vast wing span, the S.E.2010 had a bulky circular-section fuselage, with a maximum diameter of 4.7 m (15 ft 5 in). This had resulted from the initial intention of providing sleeping accommodation as an alternative to normal seating, no allowance having been made when this form of accommodation was dropped. A volume of 48 m³ (1,695 cu ft) was provided in the cargo compartments. Power was given by four 2,608 kW (3,500 hp) Pratt & Whitney R-4360-B13 Wasp Major engines, fed by eight wing fuel tanks of 31,400 litre (6,907 Imp gallon) total capacity.

The prototype was expected to be followed by a series of fifteen production Armagnacs, of which eight were for Air France and three to Transports Aériens Intercontinentaux (TAI). The last of the series was considered for use as an experimental airliner fitted with T-40 turboprop engines. The first production Armagnac flew on 30 December 1950, and by 1952 six of the first eight laid down had been delivered, four to TAI. It was in fact this airline that inaugurated Armagnac services on 8 December 1952, Air France having refused the type. However, TAI soon found the Armagnac uneconomic to operate and within months had withdrawn it from service. Not unexpectedly, the final seven Armagnacs ordered were not built.

A new lease of life for the Armagnac came with France's military commitments in South-East Asia, when several companies formed the airline SAGETA to ferry personnel, mail and freight between France and Saigon, although not by direct route. Seven Armagnacs were operated very successfully in this role.

Below: SNCASE S.E.2010 Armagnac transporting French infantry to Viet-Nam

Bottom: SNCASE S.E.2010 Armagnac

SPACE SHUTTLE
Orbiter

USA

The Space Shuttle Orbiter is the world's first re-usable space transportation system. Rockwell International was responsible for its design, development and testing and NASA is responsible for the Space Shuttle programme.

The Orbiter spacecraft is the major component of the Shuttle system, which also includes an external propellant tank and two solid-propellant rocket boosters. The Orbiter lifts off from the launch pad vertically like a rocket, with all engines firing in both the boosters and spacecraft. At an altitude of about 43 km (27 miles) the booster stages separate and descend into the sea by parachute for recovery and reuse. Under its own power, the Orbiter then continues its journey into space, jettisoning the external fuel tank just before attaining orbit.

The Orbiter itself looks somewhat like a conventional aeroplane with small double-delta

wings. The main wing assembly is primarily a conventional aluminium alloy structure. Two-segment hydraulically-actuated elevons are incorporated into each trailing-edge, for pitch and roll control, their leading-edges using a titanium rubbing strip. Hinged panels on the wing upper surface, of titanium sandwich, are used to seal the wing/elevon gap; these are the only areas of the wing not covered by the thermal protection system. The fuselage is a conventional semi-monocoque type, constructed of aluminium alloy. The forward portion contains the crew module, the mid-fuselage portion is basically an 18.28 m (60 ft)-long cargo bay with large hinged doors, and the aft portion mounts the two 26.7 kN (6,000 lb st) Aerojet Liquid Rocket Company bi-propellant liquid rocket engines for orbital manoeuvring, the three 1,668-2,090 kN (375,000-

Right: Night photograph of the Space Shuttle Orbiter _Columbia_ on the launch pad (_NASA_)

Space Shuttle Orbiter _Enterprise_ riding pick-a-back on the Model 747 Shuttle Carrier

470,000 lb st) Rocketdyne SSME high-pressure liquid oxygen/liquid hydrogen main engines, and tail unit. About 70 per cent of the exterior of the Orbiter is covered with some 34,000 silica fibre-based quartz tiles. These give thermal protection to most of the wings, fuselage and tail areas. Much of the remaining area of the Orbiter is protected from extremes of temperature. The self-contained crew module is divided into three levels, the upper (flight deck) level with side-by-side seating for two flight officers with dual controls. Behind them are seats for one or two mission specialists. On the middle deck are seats for three more mission specialists, three bunks, a galley and a hygiene section. For rescue missions, seats for three more persons can be fitted in place of the bunks. The lower deck contains environmental control equipment and crew equipment storage.

The first Shuttle spacecraft *Enterprise* (OV-101) made its first flight on top of a specially-prepared Boeing Model 747 Shuttle carrier on 18 February 1977. On 13 August the same year it was released in the air to make an unpowered free flight. By 1978 *Enterprise* had not only completed approach and landing tests but also ground vibration tests. On 1 May 1979 it was moved to launch Complex 39, Pad A, at Kennedy Space Center, where it remained until 23 July. There it was mated with an external tank and boosters and used to check out ground support equipment, procedures and launch complex facilities.

The first operational Orbiter is *Columbia* (OV-102) which, on 12 April 1981, carried out successfully the first Shuttle mission. It returned to Earth two days, six hours, 20 minutes and 52 seconds later, making a conventional landing on its tricycle landing gear. The next Orbiter, *Challenger* (OV-103), should be ready for its maiden flight at the end of 1982. (Full details of the Space Shuttle programmes can be found in the 1981-82 *Jane's Aviation Annual*).

Space Shuttle Orbiter *Columbia* touches down

TARRANT
Tabor

UK

W.G. Tarrant was a firm of building contractors based at Byfleet, Surrey. Because of its close proximity to Brooklands, where much early flying was performed by British pioneer aviators, it was frequently asked to supply timber or carry out repairs on aeroplanes. This early involvement in aviation put Tarrant in an ideal position to supply aircraft components during the First World War.

Towards the end of the war Tarrant designed a bomber of its own, with collaboration from the Royal Aircraft Establishment at Farnborough. Known as the Tabor, it was a giant triplane powered by six 373 kW (500 hp) Napier Lion engines, the lower four mounted as tandem pairs. Expected to be able to raid Berlin from bases in the UK, the single prototype was constructed at Farnborough in a disused balloon shed. But even

in this massive building the Tabor had to be constructed sideways, being removed from the shed, when completed, on railway bogies.

Apart from its size and engine/wing layout, the most interesting feature of the Tabor was its novel wooden girder contruction, which emulated the latest metal structures in material distribution. Warren-type girders formed the wing spars, tailplane spars, fuselage longerons and formers. The circular-section semi-monocoque fuselage used a two-ply skin, screwed to the longerons, formers and rings and covered with fabric, varnished and enamelled, and was positioned between the lower and middle wings. Six wheels formed the main landing gear units, three under each lower engine installation. A crew of five was expected, and the designed bomb load was 2,109 kg (4,650 lb), including release gear. The Tabor was not ready before the Armistice, but on 26 May 1919 it was prepared for its maiden flight. The pilot and co-pilot sat high in the nose well forward of the wings, a position from which they had an excellent view for take off and landing. However, when the two upper engines were opened up for take off the Tabor nosed-over, killing both pilots.

Tarrant Tabor

TUPOLEV
ANT-20 Maxim Gorki

USSR

When the Maxim Gorki first flew, on 19 May 1934, it was the largest landplane in the world. Powered by eight 671 kW (900 hp) M-34FRN engines, three in each wing leading-edge and two in tandem above the fuselage, it had huge 63 m (206 ft 8 in)-span wings of all-metal construction, the roots of which were of the same depth as the all-metal fuselage. This aircraft was used for

Above: Tupolev ANT-20 *Maxim Gorki*

Below: Tupolev ANT-20*bis* (*Planet News*)

propaganda purposes, having a wireless station, printing press and film equipment in the fuselage cabins, and illuminating equipment under the wings for displaying slogans while airborne.

In May 1935 Maxim Gorki was destroyed in a collision, with heavy loss of life. Developed from it was the ANT-20*bis* (PS-124) airliner, powered by six 932 kW (1,250 hp) engines in the wings. Accommodation was provided for a crew of eight and 60 passengers, sixteen passengers in four cabins in the wing centre-section.

This first went into service on the Moscow-Mineralnye Vody route in 1940. According to *Jane's All the World's Aircraft*, sixteen ANT-20*bis* airliners were under construction in the mid-1930s, and these were finally used as military transports during the Second World War.

TUPOLEV
TB-3 (ANT-6)

USSR

Between the two world wars the Soviet heavy bomber force was second to none – the twin-engined TB-1 had seen to this. But even while the TB-1 was in production, the first TB-3s began rolling off production lines, a new and much larger bomber powered initially by four 507 kW (680 hp) M-17F engines. During the production run of the TB-3, which lasted until 1938, by which time the aircraft was totally obsolete by modern standards, more than eight hundred were built. The design was under constant revision: the initial engines gave way to M-34s, M-34Rs, M-34RNs and R-34RNFs, corrugated-metal skins gave way to smooth skins, and other changes were made.

The prototype ANT-6 first flew in December 1930, powered by US Curtiss Conqueror engines.

Production aircraft appeared in 1932, defensively armed with ten 7.62 mm machine-guns and retaining the TB-1-type of open cockpit for the pilots. Subsequent improvements in armament included the use of manually-operated nose and dorsal gun turrets on late production aircraft. TB-3s were used in action against the Japanese in the late 1930s and again during the 'Winter War' with Finland. It was still operated as a night bomber under extreme pressure in 1941, although by then its main function was that of a troop/paratroop transport designated G-2.

An interesting use of the TB-3 was in the Zveno parasite fighter experiments, begun by the TB-1, in which two Polikarpov I-5 fighters were carried on and launched from above the wings, and two I-16 fighters were carried/launched from beneath.

Overleaf: **Tupolev TB-3s** (*W. Klepacki*)

Below: **Tupolev TB-3 being used for paratroop training** (*Imperial War Museum*)

TUPOLEV
Tu-114

USSR

When the Tu-114 went into service it was the largest and heaviest commercial airliner in the world. It appeared in 1957, and received the name *Rossiya* (Russia) to mark the 40th anniversary of the Russian Revolution. Like many previous airliners from around the world, it made use of components from a bomber, this time the wings, tail unit, landing gear and Kuznetsov NK-12MV turboprop engines of the Tu-95.

The standard version was the Tu-114, which entered service on Aeroflot's Moscow-Khabarovsk route on 24 April 1961. Normal accommodation was for 120-170 passengers, but up to 220 could be carried. This was followed by the Tu-114D, which was basically similar but had a shorter and slimmer fuselage and was intended to carry a small number of passengers, mail and urgent freight over very long distances. It is thought that about 20 Tu-114s went into service.

The prototype Tu-114D made a non-stop flight of 8,500 km (5,280 miles) from Moscow to Irkutsk and back in the spring of 1958, averaging an impressive 800 km/h (497 mph). On 24 March 1960 a Tu-114 achieved a speed of 871.38 km/h (541.45 mph) over a 1,000 km closed circuit, carrying a 25,000 kg payload. This flight set up eight official records for speeds with various payloads and for speed without payload. Other records followed, crowned on 21 April 1962 when it made a clean sweep of all the distance-with-payload records for propeller-driven aircraft, by averaging 737.352 km/h (458.2 mph) over a 10,000 km closed circuit, setting up new records for speed without payload and in the 1,000, 2,000, 5,000 and 10,000 kg payload categories.

Below: **Tupolev Tu-114 *Rossiya***

Bottom: **Tupolev Tu-114 *Rossiya***

TUPOLEV
Tu-95 and Tu-142

USSR

Soviet equivalent of the US Boeing B-52 Strato-fortress, the Tu-95 used by the strategic bomber force carries the NATO reporting name *Bear*, as does its anti-submarine warfare naval counter-part, the Tu-142. About 113 strategic bombers and 75 naval aircraft remain operational, each powered by four 11,033 kW (14,795 ehp) Kuznet-sov NK-12MV turboprop engines, driving eight-blade contra-rotating propellers.

The basic bomber version, first flown in 1954, is known to NATO as *Bear-A*. It has internal stowage for two nuclear or a variety of conven-tional free-fall weapons, and has three pairs of 23 mm cannon in remotely-controlled dorsal and ventral barbettes and a manned tail gun turret.

Bear-B, first seen during the 1961 Aviation Day

flypast, is similar to *Bear-A*, but is able to carry under its fuselage one of two large air-to-surface missiles known to NATO as *Kangaroo* and *Kitchen*. However, it is known that a small number of *Bear-Bs* also operate in a maritime reconnaissance role.

The first maritime patrol version was *Bear-C*, while *Bear-D* also has the function of providing data on the location and nature of potential targets to missile launch crews on board ships and aircraft which are themselves too distant from the target to ensure precise aiming and guidance of their surface-to-surface or air-to-surface mis-siles. About forty *Bear-Ds* are operated by the Soviet Naval air fleet.

Bear-E, another naval version, is basically similar to *Bear-A* but has the refuelling probe and rear fuselage blister fairings of *Bear-C*. It is used for maritime reconnaissance. The final version is *Bear-F*, first identified in 1973 as a much-refined anti-submarine aircraft. It has two stores bays in its rear fuselage, one of them replacing the usual rear ventral gun turret and leaving the tail turret as the sole defensive gun position. About thirty are operational.

Tu-142s have made many reconnaissance flights over US naval vessels and have been encountered frequently over the North Sea by the RAF and Royal Navy and off the US east coast.

Above right: Tupolev Tu-142 (Bear-D)

Below right: Tupolev Tu-142 (Bear-D) being escorted away from USS *Kitty Hawk* by US Navy McDonnell Douglas F-4J Phantom II fighters (*US Navy*)

Below: Tupolev Tu-142 (Bear-D)

ZEPPELIN LINDAU
Rs.I and Rs.II

Germany

As mentioned in the Zeppelin Staaken R series entry, the Count von Zeppelin authorised the construction of a huge flying-boat as the Rs.I, the design of which had been entrusted to Dipl Ing Claude Dornier. This young designer, later famed for his interwar flying-boats and warplanes of the Second World War, worked on Zeppelin projects through the affiliated Friedrichshafen Flugzeugbau. This company, formed in 1912 and the first German aircraft works devoted exclusively to the development of seaplanes, later turned also to the design and construction of landplane bombers.

Influenced perhaps by Curtiss flying-boats, the Rs.I was a giant biplane. Power was provided by three 179 kW (240 hp) Maybach Mb.IV engines installed in the hull, which drove three pusher propellers. Construction was conventional except for its copious use of metal, with a duralumin hull and a steel wing structure, fabric covered.

Construction of the Rs.I at Reutin was concurrent with the V.G.O.I. landplane bomber, and was launched on 12 October 1915. However, it was destroyed on 22 December before a flight could be made.

A follow-on flying-boat was the Rs.II, first flown on 30 June 1918. It was basically a sesquiplane, with an uncovered girder-type rear fuselage boom and twin vertical tails. Power was eventually provided by four Maybach engines in tandem pairs. After flight trials the Rs.II was dismantled. Wing span was a little over 33.2 m (108 ft).

Zeppelin Lindau Rs.II seen during flight trials (*Pilot Press*)

ZEPPELIN STAAKEN
R series

Germany

During the First World War, thirty-two Zeppelin R series heavy bombers were built at the Staaken works, only a few of which were brought down in action. Some of the remaining aircraft were peacefully employed after the end of the war, giving seaside joyrides and weekend flights from Berlin to the Baltic and North Sea.

Although it is generally believed that German heavy bombers were conceived after years of war, the facts are very different. In the first month of war, in 1914, Count von Zeppelin (famed for his airships) requested giant aeroplanes to be designed, entrusting to Dipl Ing Claude Dornier the huge metal naval aircraft, and to Prof Baumann a machine of one ton carrying capacity capable of a 700 km return flight. The flying-boat became the Zeppelin Lindau Rs I. Design of the landplane bomber by Prof Baumann, with assistance from Hellmuth Hirth and Klein, was started in September 1914 (partly financed by the Bosch Magneto Company, who also supplied four draughtsmen) and completed by the end of the same year. Without delay construction of a prototype was put in hand, but progress was slowed down by the late delivery of the three 179 kW (240 hp) Maybach engines.

Known as the V.G.O. I, the bomber first flew on 11 April 1915 from the Gotha works, specially hired for the purpose. Unfortunately the engines played up, and so in May the giant was flown to Friedrichshafen for repairs. It was not until autumn that the bomber was again ready for flight, but on its return trip to Gotha it ran into a snowstorm, causing the engines to fail. The pilot, Hellmuth Hirth, executed a forced landing in a wooded valley which, although saving the crew, wrecked the bomber.

Zeppelin Staaken R.VI

So well had the bomber flown up to the time of the accident that it was decided to rebuild it, later being sent for trials to the Eastern Front. Flown there by the German Navy, it performed many raids before returning to Germany for further trials. But its return also marked its demise, for while it was being flown by Klein it crashed, killing him and one other person.

Whatever the circumstances of the V.G.O.I's accident, it had proved the basic concept. From this bomber was, therefore, evolved the V.G.O.II and V.G.O.III (R.II and R.III), powered by five Maybach and six 119 kW (160 hp) D.III engines respectively. The former crashed before delivery to the Army, but the R.III was flown on the Eastern Front. Not deterred, a single R.IV followed, powered by four 164 kW (220 hp) Benz Bz.IV and two 119 kW (160 hp) Mercedes D.IIIs, and the R.V. of 1916 with five Mb.IV engines. The R.V. had much better performance than the R.IV, including a service ceiling of 4,000 m (13,125 ft), 1,000 m higher than the R.IV's.

Up to this point the bombers had been single prototypes, but the R.VI changed this. Powered by four 194 kW (260 hp) Mercedes D.IVa or Mb.IV engines, eighteen were built by Zeppelin, Albatros, Aviatik and Schütte-Lanz from 1916 until the end of the war. R.VIs were armed with four Parabellum machine-guns and eighteen 100 kg bombs. Apart from its huge size and tandem engine arrangement, it was unusual in that its main landing gear units had no less than sixteen wheels, grouped in fours, as well as a further two wheels under the nose. A number of R.VIs took part in attacks on French and British targets.

Meanwhile, in 1917 the one-off R.VII appeared, followed by three R.XIVs with five Mb.IV engines each, one R.XIVa and three R.XVs with five Mb.IV engines each. The final landplane bomber of the series was the R.XVI, powered by two Benz Bz.IV and two 410 kW (550 hp) Benz Bz.VI engines, although a handful of similar seaplanes were also completed.

ZEPPELIN-STAAKEN
E.4/20 Giant

Germany

Although the provisions of the Treaty of Versailles restrained the construction of airships, Zeppelin and its branches were by no means idle postwar. Some branches took up the construction of motorboats and other non-aviation products, while at others aviation work continued. The Seemoos factory remained an experimental establishment under Dr Dornier, but at the Staaken works near Berlin a new four-engined high-wing monoplane airliner was produced, just one of five new civil aircraft Zeppelin Werke built up to the time of the prohibition of construction.

The E.4/20 Giant (popular name) had a fuselage constructed of riveted duralumin sheet over duralumin girder bulkheads. Interestingly, no longerons were used. The main cabin accommodated eighteen passengers, who entered via a ladder through the hinged nose. Pilot and co-pilot sat above the cabin in an open cockpit. Perhaps the most impressive feature of the aircraft was its semi-cantilever monoplane wing, built out from specially heavy bulkheads in the fuselage. They were of deep section, no less than 1.2 m (4 ft) at the roots, and were constructed using duralumin spars and ribs, the duralumin skin forming an integral part of the structure. Into the wings were built four nacelles for the 183 kW (245 hp) Maybach engines, each nacelle with a seat for a mechanic. These seats could be reached from the fuselage by crawling through a tunnel in the wings. The main landing gear was simplicity itself, with three struts each side, two horizontal and one vertical, and each unit carrying twin wheels.

Designed in 1919 by Dipl Ing Adolf Rohrbach, best known for his large flying-boats of the latter 1920s, construction was mainly carried out during 1920. Intended to be used on commercial services between Friedrichshafen and Berlin, it was rolled out in September and thereafter flew successfully on test until grounded prematurely by the Control Commission. The aircraft's ignominious end came in November 1922, when it was scrapped.

Zeppelin Staaken E.4/20 Giant

AIRCRAFT SPECIFICATION
TABLES

Aircraft specification relates to the particular version detailed	Wing span metres (feet)	Length overall metres (feet)	Height overall metres (feet)	Maximum T-O weight kg (lb)	Maximum speed knots (km/h; mph)	Cruising speed at optimum altitude knots (km/h; mph)	Range/ endurance range in nm (km; miles)	Remarks
AEG R.I	36.00 (118-1¼)	20.00 (65-7½)	—	12,500 (27,557)	—	—	—	Disposable load, except for 2,750 litres (605 Imp gals) fuel, was about 3.7 tons
Aero Spacelines Guppy-201	47.62 (156-3)	43.84 (143-10)	14.78 (48-6)	77,110 (170,000)	250 (463;288)	220 (407;253)	*440 (813;505)	*With maximum payload
Airbus A300B4-200	44.84 (147-1)	53.62 (175-11)	16.53 (54-2¾)	142,000 (313,055)	*345 (639;397)	492 (911;567)	ø2,750 (5,095; 3,165)	*CAS ø With 269 passengers
Antonov An-22	64.40 (211-4)	57.80 (189-7)	12.53 (41-1½)	250,000 (551,160)	399 (740;460)	—	*2,692 (5,000; 3,100)	*With max payload
Barling XNBL-1	36.58 (120-0)	19.81 (65-0)	8.53 (28-0)	19,309 (42,569)	83 (154;96)	53 (98;61)	148 (274;170)	Maximum bomb-load 2,268 kg (5,000 lb)
Beardmore Inflexible	48.00 (157-6)	23.0 (75-6)	6.45 (21-2)	16,783 (37,000)	95 (175;109)	—	—	
Blackburn B-101 Beverley	49.38 (162-0)	30.30 (99-5)	11.71 (38-5)	61,235 (135,000)	207 (383;238)	152 (283;175)	*174 (322;200)	*With max payload
Blohm und Voss Bv 222C	46.00 (150-11)	37.00 (121-4¾)	10.90 (35-9¼)	48,980 (107,982)	210 (390;242)	186 (345;214)	3,291 (6,100; 3,790)	
Blohm und Voss Bv 238V-1	60.15 (197-4)	43.50 (142-8½)	13.40 (43-11½)	80,000 (176,370)	229 (425;264)	—	2,080 (3,855; 2,395)	
Boeing B-29B Superfortress	43.05 (141-3)	30.18 (99-0)	9.02 (29-7)	62,369 (137,500)	*316 (586;364)	198 (367;228)	3,647 (6,759; 4,200)	*At 7,620 m (25,000 ft)
Boeing B-50A Superfortress	43.05 (141-3)	30.18 (99-0)	9.96 (32-8)	78,471 (173,000)	*334 (620;385)	204 (378;235)	4,038 (7,483; 4,650)	*At 7,620 m (25,000 ft)
Boeing B-52H Stratofortress	56.39 (185-0)	47.55 (156-0)	12.40 (40-8)	221,353 (488,000)	*547 (1,014;630)	491 (909;565)	10,855 (20,117; 12,500)	*At 12,190 m (40,000 ft)
Boeing Model 314A	46.33 (152-0)	32.31 (106-0)	6.21 (20-4½)	38,102 (84,000)	173 (320;199)	—	4,516 (8,369; 5,200)	
Boeing Model 707-320C	44.42 (145-9)	46.61 (152-11)	12.93 (42-5)	151,315 (333,600)	545 (1,010;627)	478 (886;550)	*5,000 (9,265; 5,755)	*With 147 passengers
Boeing Model 747-200B	59.64 (195-8)	70.66 (231-10)	19.33 (63-5)	377,840 (833,000)	*523 (969;602)	—	ø5,700 (10,562; 6,563)	*At 9,145 m (30,000 ft) ø At max T-O weight, with 442 passengers
Boeing XB-15	45.42 (149-0)	26.70 (83-7)	5.51 (18-1)	32,072 (70,706)	174 (322;200)	—	4,455 (8,256; 5,130)	

Aircraft specification relates to the particular version detailed	Wing span metres (feet)	Length overall metres (feet)	Height overall metres (feet)	Maximum T-O weight kg (lb)	Maximum speed knots (km/h; mph)	Cruising speed at optimum altitude knots (km/h; mph)	Range/endurance range in nm (km; miles)	Remarks
Bordelaise D.B.71	37.00 (121-4¾)	20.00 (65-7½)	6.00 (19-8)	13,250 (29,211)	119 (220;137)	107 (200;123)	—	The A.B.20 bomber was larger and heavier than the D.B.71
Breguet 521 Bizerte	35.13 (115-3)	20.30 (66-7¼)	7.60 (24-11¼)	16,500 (35,274)	138 (255;159)	—	1,133 (2,100; 1,305)	
Breguet Type 765 Sahara	43.00 (141-0¾)	28.94 (94-11¼)	10.15 (33-3½)	54,000 119,050)	—	205 (380;236)	2,536 (4,700; 2,290)	
Bristol Brabazon I	70.10 (230-0)	53.95 (177-0)	15.24 (50-0)	131.542 (290,000)	261 (483;300)	217 (402;250)	*4,776 (8,851; 5,500)	*Estimated
Cameron Balloons A.530	*34.44 (113-0)	—	54.86 (180-0)	—	—	—	—	*Diameter of balloon envelope
Caproni Ca 90P.B	46.56 (152-9)	26.92 (88-4)	10.81 (35-5½)	30,000 (66,138)	110 (205;127)	—	Endurance 7 hours	
Caproni Triple Hydro-Triplane	33.00 (108-3)	22.00 (72-2¼)	9.60 (31-6)	25,000 (55,115)	78 (145;90)	—	Endurance 6 hours	With 100 passengers
Cierva W.11 Air Horse	*28.96 (95-0)	ø27.00 (88-7)	5.41 (17-9)	7,938 (17,500)	122 (225;140)	82 (153;95)	287 (531;330)	*Width overall rotors turning ø Length overall rotors turning
Consolidated B-32 Dominator	41.15 (135-0)	25-32 (83-1)	9.80 (32-2)	54,431 (120,000)	*313 (579;360)	—	ø695 (1,287; 800)	*At 7,620 m (25,000 ft) ø With max bombload
Consolidated PB2Y-3 Coronado	35.05 (115-0)	24.16 (79-3)	8.38 (27-6)	30,844 (68,000)	*185 (343;213)	122 (227;141)	1,294 (2,398; 1,490)	*At 6,100 m (20,000 ft)
Consolidated Vultee B-36D	70.10 (230-0)	49.40 (162-1)	14.22 (46-8)	162,159 (357,500)	*381 (707;439)	195 (362;225)	6,513 (12,070; 7,500)	*At 9,785 m (32,100 ft)
Consolidated XC-99	70.10 (230-0)	55.63 (182-6)	17.53 (57-6)	145,150 (320,000)	261 (483;300)	—	7,034 (13,035; 8,100)	
Convair R3Y-2 Tradewind	44.20 (145-0)	43.43 (142-6)	—	79,379 (175,000)	*304 (563;350)	261 (483;300)	3,474 (6,437; 4,000)	*At 7,620 m (25,000 ft)
Dornier Do X	48.0 (157-5¾)	40.05 (131-4¾)	9.00 (29-6¼)	56,000 (123,460)	116 (216;134)	102 (190;118)	916 (1,700; 1,055)	
Douglas C-124C Globemaster II	53.07 (174-1½)	39.75 (130-5)	14.72 (48-3½)	88,224 (194,500)	*235 (436;271)	200 (370;230)	ø3,500 (6,486; 4,030)	*At sea level ø With 10,739 kg (26,375 lb) payload

Aircraft specification relates to the particular version detailed	Wing span metres (feet)	Length overall metres (feet)	Height overall metres (feet)	Maximum T-O weight kg (lb)	Maximum speed knots (km/h; mph)	Cruising speed at optimum altitude knots (km/h; mph)	Range/ endurance range in nm (km; miles)	Remarks
Douglas C-133B Cargomaster	54.76 (179-8)	48.02 (157-6½)	14.71 (48-3)	136,078 (300,000)	*301 (558;347)	269 (499;310)	ø1,954 (3,621; 2,250)	* At 2,740 m (9,000 ft) ø With 41,386 kg (91,240 lb) payload
Douglas XB-19	64.62 (212-0)	40.34 (132-4)	—	73,482 (162,000)	195 (360;224)	—	6,696 (12,408; 7,710)	
Farman F.222	36.00 (118-1¼)	21.57 (70-9¼)	5.19 (17-0½)	18,700 (41,226)	175 (325;202)	—	647 (1,200; 745)	Could carry 4,430 kg (9,771 lb) bombload
Focke Achgelis Fa 223E Drache	*24.50 (80-4½)	12.25 (40-2¼)	4.36 (14-3¾)	5,000 (11,023)	ø64 (120;74)	64 (120;74)	†378 (700;435)	* Width overall, rotors turning ø Limited by rotor vibration † With auxiliary fuel
Focke-Wulf Fw 200C-3 Condor	32.85 (107-9¼)	23.85 (78-3)	6.30 (20-8)	22,700 (50,045)	*195 (360;224)	ø181 (335;208)	1,921 (3,560; 2,212)	* At 4,700 m (15,420 ft) ø At 4,000 m (13,125 ft)
General Aircraft Hamilcar	33.53 (110-0)	20.73 (68-0)	6.17 (20-3)	16,329 (36,000)	*130 (241;150)	—	—	* Maximum towed speed
Handley Page V/1500	38.40 (126-0)	18.90 (62-0)	7.01 (23-0)	11,204 (24,700)	*84 (156;97)	—	Max endurance 14 hours	* At 2,665 m (8,750 ft)
Handley Page Victor B.Mk2	36.58 (120-0)	35.03 (114-11)	9.18 (30-1½)	79,379 (175,000)	*556 (1,030; 640)	—	3,995 (7,403; 4,600)	* At 12,190 m (40,000 ft)
Heinkel He 111Z-1	35.20 (115-6)	17.50 (57-5)	4.40 (14-5¼)	28,500 (62,832)	*76 (140;87)	—	—	* With an Me 321 in tow at 4,000 m (13,125 ft)
Heinkel He 177A-5 Greif	31.44 (103-1¾)	19.40 (63-7¾)	6.40 (21-00)	31,000 (68,343)	*263 (488;303)	225 (415;259)	ø2,968 (5,500; 3,418)	* At 6,000 m (19,685 ft) ø With two Hs 293 missiles
Heinkel He 274V-1	44.20 (145-0¼)	23.80 (78-1)	5.50 (18-0½)	36,000 (79,366)	*313 (580;360)	216 (400;249)	1,538 (2,850; 1,771)	* At 11,000 m (36,090 ft)
Hughes H-4 Hercules	97.536 (320-0)	66.75 (219-0)	—	181,436 (400,000)	—	*174 (322;200)	—	* Estimated
Hughes XH-17	*39.62 (130-0)	—	ø9.14 (30-0)	19,960 (43,000)	—	—	—	* Rotor diameter ø More than
Hurel-Dubois H.D.321	45.30 (148-7½)	23.27 (76-4¼)	8.73 (28-7¾)	18,700 (41,226)	—	148 (275;171)	1,187 (2,200; 1,367)	
I.A.38	32.00 (105-0)	13.50 (44-3½)	4.60 (15-1)	16,000 (35,274)	*135 (252;156)	*116 215;134)	674 (1,250; 776)	* Estimated. Crew of two in compartment over wing leading-edge

Aircraft specification relates to the particular version detailed	Wing span metres (feet)	Length overall metres (feet)	Height overall metres (feet)	Maximum T-O weight kg (lb)	Maximum speed knots (km/h; mph)	Cruising speed at optimum altitude knots (km/h; mph)	Range/ endurance range in nm (km; miles)	Remarks
Ilyushin Il-76T	50.50 (165-8)	46.59 (152-10½)	14.76 (48-5)	170,000 (374,785)	459 (850;528)	405 (750;466)	*2,700 (5,000; 3,100)	*With max payload
Ilyushin Il-86	48.06 (157-8¼)	60.21 (197-6½)	15.68 (51-5½)	206,000 (454,150)	—	*512 (950;590)	ø1,944 (3,600; 2,235)	*9,000-11,000 m (30,000-36,000 ft) ø With max payload
Junkers G38	44.00 (144-4)	23.20 (76-1)	6.50 (21-4)	24,000 (52,911)	—	110 (208;127)	1,889 (3,500; 2,175)	
Junkers Ju 322V-1	62.00 (203-5)	30.25 (99-3)	—	*11,000 (24,250)	—	—	—	*Approximate payload
Junkers Ju 390A-1	50.30 (165-0¼)	34.00 (111-6½)	6.90 (22-7½)	*75,500 (166,450)	*273 (505;314)	—	*5,234 (9,700; 6,027)	*Estimated figures
Junkers Mistel 3C Composite	20.08 (65-10½)	*18.54 (60-10)	—	23,600 (52,029)	ø297 (550;342)	ø173 (320;199)	ø2,213 (4,100; 2,548	*Including warhead ø Approximate figures
Kamov Ka 22 Vintokryl	*28.05 (92-0¼)	22.50 (73-9¾)	8.25 (27-0¾)	33,700 (74,296)	ø203 (377;234)	—	—	*Width overall, rotors turning ø At sea level
Kawanishi H6K5	40.00 (131-2¾)	25.63 (84-1)	6.27 (20-6¾)	23,000 (50,706)	208 (385;239)	140 (260;161)	3,656 (6,775; 4,210)	
Kawanishi H8K2	38.00 (124-8)	28.13 (92-3½)	9.15 (30-0¼)	32,500 (71,650)	251 (465;289)	159 (295;183)	3,858 (7,150; 4,443)	
Latécoère 521	49.30 (161-9)	31.62 (103-8¾)	9.07 (29-9)	37,000 (81,570)	141 (262;162)	124 (230;143)	*2,212 (4,100; 2,547)	*Max range. Latécoère 522 and 523 each had max T-O weight of 42,000 kg (92,594 lb)
Latécoère 631	57.43 (188-5)	43.46 (142-7)	10.35 (33-11½)	75,000 (165,347)	234 (435;270)	173 (320;199)	3,270 (6,060; 3,766)	Crew of 9 and 40 or more passengers Data applies to higher-powered boats
Lawson L-4	33.96 (111-5)	16.51 (54-2)	5.33 (17-6)	8,457 (18,645)	96 (177;110)	—	738 (1,368; 850)	Twenty-four passengers
Linke-Hoffmann R.I	33.20 (108-11)	15.60 (51-2¼)	6.70 (21-11¾)	11,200 (24,692)	70 (130;81)	—	Endurance 5 hours	
Lockheed C-141A Starlifter	48.80 (160-1)	44.20 (145-0)	11.98 (39-3½)	143,607 (316,600)	495 (917;570)	426 (788;490)	*3,856 (7,145; 4,440)	*With 31,071 kg (68,500 lb) payload
Lockheed C-5A Galaxy	67.88 (222-8½)	75.54 (247-10)	19.85 (65-1½)	348,813 (769,000)	*496 (919;571)	450 (834;518)	ø3,256 (6,033; 3,749)	*At 7,620 m (25,000 ft) ø With 100,228 kg (220,967 lb) payload

Aircraft specification relates to the particular version detailed	Wing span metres (feet)	Length overall metres (feet)	Height overall metres (feet)	Maximum T-O weight kg (lb)	Maximum speed knots (km/h; mph)	Cruising speed at optimum altitude knots (km/h; mph)	Range/endurance range in nm (km; miles)	Remarks
Lockheed 1649A Starliner	45.72 (150-0)	*35.41 (116-2)	7.14 (23-5)	70,760 (156,000)	ø327 (607;377)	297 (550;342)	6,253 (11,587; 7,200)	*With weather radar ø At 5,670 m (18,600 ft)
Lockheed R60-1 Constitution	57.63 (189-1)	47.57 (156-1)	15.35 (50-4½)	83,461 (184,000)	*263 (488;303)	248 (460;286)	5,471 (10,139; 6,300)	*At 6,100 m (20,000 ft)
MacCready Solar Challenger	14.33 (47-0)	9.27 (30-5)	1.94 (6-4½)	160 (353)	30.5 (56.5;35)	*61 (113;70)	ø260 (483;300)	*Max cruising speed at 9,145 m (30,000 ft) ø Limited by duration and intensity of sun
Martin Model 156	47.85 (157-0)	27.99 (91-10)	7.47 (24-6)	28,576 (63,000)	*165 (306;190)	135 (251;156)	2,093 (3,879; 2,410)	*At 1,770 m (5,800 ft)
Martin XP6M-1 Seamaster	30.48 (100-0)	40.84 (134-0)	9.45 (31-0)	*13,608 (30,000)	521 (966;600)	—	—	*Max payload
Martin JRM-1 Mars	60.96 (200-0)	36.65 (120-3)	13.59 (44-7)	65,771 (145,000)	193 (357;222)	133 (246;153)	—	
Maxim 1894 Biplane	31.70 (104-0)	36.58 (120-0)	—	*3,629 (8,000)	—	—	—	*Max loaded weight of test rig
McDonnell Douglas DC-8 Super 63	45.23 (148-5)	57.12 (187-5)	12.92 (42-5)	158,757 (350,000)	*521 (965;600)	—	6,686 (12,390; 7,700)	*Max recommended cruising speed at 9,145 m (30,000 ft)
Messerschmitt Me 264 V-3	43.00 (141-1)	20.90 (68-6¾)	—	56,040 (123,547)	—	188 (350;217)	8,095 (15,000; 9,321)	
Messerschmitt Me 323D-6 Gigant	55.00 (180-5¼)	28.15 (92-4¼)	—	43,000 (94,799)	*154 (285;177)	*117 (218;135)	594 (1,100; 684)	*At sea level
Mil Mi-26	*32.00 (105-0)	ø33.73 (110-8)	—	56,000 (123,450)	—	137 (255;158)	432 (800;497)	*Rotor diameter ø Length of fuselage
Mil V-12	*35.00 (114-10)	ø37.00 (121-4½)	12.50 (41-0)	105,000 (231,500)	140 (260;161)	130 (240;150)	269 (500;310)	*Rotor diameter ø Length of fuselage
Myasishchev M-4 *Bison-A*	50.48 (165-7½)	47.20 (154-10)	—	158,750 (350,000)	486 (900;560)	—	6,079 (11,250; 7,000)	
North American XB-70A Valkyrie	32.00 (105-0)	59.74 (196-0)	—	—	Mach 3.0	Mach 3.0	*6,600 (12,230; 7,600)	*Approximately

Aircraft specification relates to the particular version detailed	Wing span metres (feet)	Length overall metres (feet)	Height overall metres (feet)	Maximum T-O weight kg (lb)	Maximum speed knots (km/h; mph)	Cruising speed at optimum altitude knots (km/h; mph)	Range/endurance range in nm (km; miles)	Remarks
Northrop B-35	52.43 (172-0)	16.18 (53-1)	6.12 (20-1)	94,800 (209,000)	434 (805;500)	—	—	A YB-49 flew 5,565 km (3,458 miles) at an average cruising speed of 615 km/h (382 mph)
Penhoët Flying-Boat	40.0 (131-3)	27.0 (88-7)	7.75 (25-5)	16,000 (35,275)	*86 (160;99)	—	—	*Estimated
Piasecki Pv-15 Transporter	*25.00 (82-0)	ø23.77 (78-0)	7.62 (25-0)	†13,608 (30,000)	†109 (201;125)	—	†174 (322;200)	*Rotor diameter ø Length of fuselage † More than
R101 Airship	NA	220.68 (724-0)	42.67 (140-0)	*123,957 (273,280)	ø69 (129;80)	ø61 (113;70)	ø2,605 (4,828; 3,000)	*Approximate empty weight. Max lift 153,423 kg (338,240 lb) ø Approximate figures
Rockwell International B-1	41.67 (136-8½)	45.78 (150-2½)	10.24 (33-7¼)	179,170 (395,000)	*Mach 2.2	563 (1,042; 648)	Intercontinental	*Approximately
Saunders-Roe Princess	*66.90 (219-6)	45.11 (148-0)	16.99 (55-9)	149,685 (330,000)	—	313 (579;360)	4,577 (8,481; 5,270)	*With wingtip floats up. Span with wingtip floats down 64.16 m (210 ft 6 in)
Shin Meiwa PS-1	33.15 (108-9)	33.46 (109-9¼)	*9.82 (32-4¾)	43,000 (94,800)	295 (547;340)	230 (426;265)	ø1,170 (2,168; 1,347)	*On beaching gear ø Endurance 15 hours
Short Cromarty	34.59 (113-6)	17.98 (59-0)	7.01 (23-0)	8,981 (19,800)	83 (154;96)	78 (145;90)	*860 (1,593; 990)	*Max range. Operated by crew of three
Short Kent	34.44 (113-0)	23.90 (78-5)	8.53 (28-0)	14,515 (32,000)	119 (220;137)	91 (169;105)	391 (724;450)	Fifteen passengers
Short-Mayo Composite	*22.25 (73-0) ø34.75 (114-0)	*15.52 (50-11) ø25.88 (84-11)	*6.17 (20-3) ø9.94 (32-7½)	†22,135 (48,800)	ø184 (341;212)	†202 (233;145)	ø3,387 (6,276; 3,900)	*Mercury ø Maia † Composite of both
Short Sarafand	36.58 (120-0)	27.25 (89-5)	*10.21 (33-6)	31,751 (70,000)	133 (246;153)	—	1,259 (2,334; 1,450)	Crew of ten *On beaching gear
Short Shetland II	45.82 (150-4)	32.92 (108-0)	11.79 (38-8)	58,967 (130,000)	232 (430;267)	—	*2,605 (4,828; 3,000)	*With a 9,979 kg (22,000 lb) payload
Short Belfast	48.40 (158-9½)	41.58 (136-5)	14.33 (47-0)	102,058 (225,000)	Mach 0.65	306 (566;352)	4,603 (8,530; 5,300)	Heavy lift Belfasts can carry 34,000 kg (75,000 lb) of freight

Aircraft specification relates to the particular version detailed	Wing span metres (feet)	Length overall metres (feet)	Height overall metres (feet)	Maximum T-O weight kg (lb)	Maximum speed knots (km/h; mph)	Cruising speed at optimum altitude knots (km/h; mph)	Range/endurance range in nm (km; miles)	Remarks
Siemens-Schuckert R.I	28.00 (91-10¼)	17.50 (57-5)	5.20 (17-0¾)	5,200 (11,464)	59 (110;68)	—	Endurance 4 hours	
Sikorsky *Le Grand*	28.00 (91-10¼)	20.00 (65-7½)	—	*4,080 (9,000)	—	*48 (88;55)	—	*Approximate figures. Wing span of *Ilya Mourometz* Type B was 31.00 (101-8½)
SNCASE S.E.2010 Armagnac	48.95 (160-7¼)	39.63 (130-0¼)	13.50 (44-3½)	77,500 (170,858)	286 (530;329)	244 (452;281)	2,762 (5,120; 3,181)	
Space Shuttle Orbiter	23.79 (78-0¾)	37.19 (122-0¼)	17.25 (56-7)	*96,162 (212,000)	ø15,284 (28,325; 17,600)	—	—	*Designed landing weight with a 14,515 kg (32,000 lb) payload. Orbiter can carry up to 29,484 kg (65,000 lb) cargo into earth orbit ø Orbital speed
Tarrant Tabor	40.00 (131-3)	22.30 (73-2)	11.35 (37-3)	20,263 (44,672)	*99 (183;114)	—	*947 (1,754; 1,090)	*Estimated figures
Tupolev ANT-20 Maxim Gorki	63.00 (206-8)	32.90 (107-11¼)	—	42,000 (92,594)	—	119 (220;137)	648 (1,200; 746)	
Tupolev TB-3	41.80 (137-1½)	25.20 (82-8)	—	18,875 (41,612)	155 (288;179)	—	1,349 (2,500; 1,553)	
Tupolev Tu-95/Tu-142	*51.10 (167-8)	*49.50 (162-5)	*12.12 (39-9)	188,000 (414,470)	ø434 (805;500)	—	†6,774 (12,550; 7,800)	*Bear-F approximate ø Bear-A † Bear-A with 11,340 kg (25,000 lb) bombload
Tupolev Tu-114	51.10 (167-8)	54.10 (177-6)	—	171,000 (376,990)	469 (870;540)	415 (770;478)	4,828 (8,950; 5,560)	
Zeppelin Lindau Rs.I	43.5 (142-8½)	29.0 (95-1¾)	7.20 (23-7½)	10,500 (23,149)	—	—	—	
Zeppelin Staaken E.4/20 Giant	31.00 (101-8½)	16.48 (54-0¾)	5.20 (17-0¾)	8,500-9,180 (18,739-20,238)	122 (225;140)	—	594 (1,100; 684)	Eighteen passengers
Zeppelin Staaken R.VI	42.20 (138-5½)	22.10 (72-6)	6.30 (20-8)	11,850 (26,125)	70 (130;81)	—	Endurance 10 hours	